Teaching
TENACITY,
RESILIENCE,
and a
DRIVE FOR
EXCELLENCE

Teaching
TENACITY,
RESILIENCE,
and a
DRIVE FOR
EXCELLENCE

Lessons for Social-
Emotional Learning
for Grades 4–8

Emily Mofield, Ed.D., and
Megan Parker Peters, Ph.D.

PRUFROCK PRESS INC.
WACO, TEXAS

Dedication

To my mentor and friend, Kayren Craighead, for always encouraging me to have tenacity, resilience, and a drive for excellence for impacting student learning. Thank you for believing in me when I knew so little—for planting a seed and nurturing my growth! And to my family—Ashley, Ellie, Bill, and Janice—thank you for your constant love and support.

—Emily

To my parents, Randy and Charlotte, who never let me believe that anything was out of reach or impossible. Your tenacity and drive for excellence have inspired me to set and reach goals that I never thought imaginable.

—Megan

Soli deo gloria.

Prufrock Press Inc.
P.O. Box 8813
Waco, TX 76714-8813
Phone: (800) 998-2208
Fax: (800) 240-0333
http://www.prufrock.com

Table of Contents

Acknowledgements   ix

Introduction   1

Pre- and Postassessment   13

PART I: Persevering With a Passion for Learning   21

Lesson 1   Ingredients for Success   23

Lesson 2   Talent Meets Passion   29

Lesson 3   Encounters With Eminent Individuals   35

Lesson 4   The Why Factor   41

Lesson 5   Tenacity   49

Lesson 6   Grit   55

Lesson 7   Face-to-Face With Obstacles   61

Lesson 8   Deliberate Practice   71

Lesson 9   Getting in the Flow   77

PART II: Growing Toward Excellence   85

Lesson 10   Growth Mindset   87

Lesson 11   Pursuit of Excellence Versus Perfectionism   101

Lesson 12   Changing Thinking   111

Lesson 13   Facing the Fear of Failure   119

Lesson 14   Handling Mistakes   125

Lesson 15   Dealing With Setbacks   137

Lesson 16   Can Stress Lead to Success?   145

Lesson 17   From Procrastinating to Producing   153

PART III: Guiding Emotion Toward Excellence 161

    Lesson 18   Understanding Emotions 163

    Lesson 19   Managing Emotion 171

    Lesson 20   Hope and Learned Optimism 183

    Lesson 21   Self-Awareness 191

    Lesson 22   A Matter of Perspective 197

    Lesson 23   Interpersonal Problem Solving 203

    Lesson 24   Assuredly Assertive 209

References 217

Appendix: Additional Resources and Supplemental Lesson 223

About the Authors 227

NAGC Programming Standards Alignment 229

Acknowledgements

This project would not be possible without the teachers who piloted many of the lessons and gave us feedback for improvement. We especially thank the teachers of Sumner County—Ashley Kirk, Vicki Phelps, Jason Tomlinson, Ales Dvorak, Karah Lewis, and Paula Kiggins—for suggestions and insight regarding the concepts in these lessons. Thank you to Mattie Cantrell for using the lessons with younger students and offering thoughtful ideas. We also express gratitude to our editor, Katy McDowall, for believing in this project and supporting its development.

Introduction

As educators, we shape and support the growth of students. Presented with an array of student abilities, we are tasked with supporting and transforming those abilities into actualized achievement. What does it take? How can we foster resilience in the face of setbacks? How can we teach students to have tenacity as they persevere through challenges when it would be easier to give up? What gets in the way of student success, and how can we support students to problem solve with zeal instead of fear? In talent development, noncognitive skills are important factors that help thrust achievement to higher levels. In line with the importance of cultivating psychosocial skills such as tenacity, resilience, and mindset to help promote achievement (Subotnik, 2015; Subotnik, Olszewski-Kubilius, & Worrell, 2011), this curriculum is the how-to for doing so. We can help students tackle obstacles before them, reframe their thinking so that they are not discouraged from defeat, and reach and perform at the edge of their abilities.

Purpose

This curriculum fosters psychosocial skills that prepare students for long-term success. Psychosocial skills help individuals deliberately and productively achieve goals (Olszewski-Kubilius & Calvert, 2016). In the context of talent development, these skills propel a learner to the next level (potential to competence, competence to expertise, expertise to demonstrated achievement; Subotnik et al., 2011). This resource, written for students in grades 4–8, provides tools and strategies teachers can use to cultivate tenacity, emotional regulation, resilience, and a comfort with tension.

Although we wrote this resource with gifted students and their talent development in mind, these skills and strategies can support the long-term success of any student. The lessons include social-emotional concepts appropriate for all levels of learners.

Much has been discussed about grit, growth mindset, learning from failure, and overcoming obstacles. Although students may understand that mistakes help them grow and that they will need to overcome obstacles to obtain their dreams, they still experience disappointment, frustration, and fear when faced with challenges. We must teach students to deal with the unpleasant emotions that accompany setbacks. When students are working at the edge of their competencies, they are more likely to make mistakes, but they are also more likely to grow.

To teach tenacity and resilience, we must guide students to become self-aware of obstacles that may keep them from achieving their personal goals, some of which they can control and some they cannot, and how it is important to know the difference. Further, we can help develop students' sense of purpose by encouraging students to think beyond self-oriented goals and consider how they can positively contribute to change in the world. We believe that this comes through teaching students to be mindful of how they pursue excellence. We use the phrase *mindful excellence* throughout the curriculum to mean being aware of how our thoughts, emotions, and beliefs about abilities affect how we pursue developing our own unknowable potential.

How do we teach these skills in today's classrooms? Learning to persevere with sustained effort does not happen by accident. First and foremost, we must create contexts for developing academic perseverance. Tenacity, grit, and growth mindset only happen when a student has an opportunity to develop skills to work hard. Although this curriculum provides numerous engaging activities and strategies that teach students about tenacity, resilience, and self-awareness, these activities will not effectively translate to students' lives in the absence of appropriately challenging curriculum and instruction. However, we know that even when teachers are able to provide challenging content that supplies the context to nurture perseverance, teachers are still looking for direct strategies to deliberately guide students to develop these skills.

As well as explicit lessons on cultivating social-emotional skills that drive excellence, this curriculum includes opportunities (or Curriculum Extensions) for teachers to link the concepts to curriculum content. For example, students may analyze characters' thoughts and feelings and determine how they relate to perseverance, coping with stress, and emotional regulation. In other lessons, students might study eminent individuals in history, science, or math to understand the approaches they took to overcome obstacles.

This curriculum is built around the assumption that ability is important, but it alone does not lead to success. Further, motivation to succeed in the form of grit, self-discipline, or ambition does not lead to automatic success. Students must have the opportunity for *all* of these factors to be nurtured. This includes *opportunities* to work hard, apply authentic effort, practice self-regulation strategies in various domains, and develop abilities to the fullest. These self-regulation skills can only be applied when a skill feels difficult and hard; therefore, it is important to remind students that when a task feels challenging, it is an opportunity develop both the learned skill and the self-regulation skill. Through the interaction of developing both cognitive and non-cognitive factors, students can reach unknowable potential.

Teaching for Talent Development

The teaching of psychosocial skills should be matched to certain stages of talent development. For example, Olszewski-Kubilius and Calvert (2016) explained that mindset and teachability are important at the first stages of talent development when students are introduced to foundational concepts in the talent domain. In later stages, it is important to develop skills to challenge instructors and advocate for creative ideas even through criticism (Subotnik & Jarvin, 2005). In this curriculum, most lessons relate to the early stages of talent development (e.g., potential to competency), given that the lessons are for grades 4–8; however, some skills, such as using assertive communication, applying deliberate practice, and responding to criticism, can be applied throughout talent development stages.

Links to Emotional Intelligence

Emotional intelligence is particularly important, as it relates to tenacity and a pursuit of excellence. Fear is a powerful force that causes avoidance of challenges. The emotion of disappointment can paralyze one to never want to take risks. The feeling of hope can be used to catalyze momentum toward the completion of a goal. Self-regulation of emotion in high-stakes performance situations is important for long-term success (Olszewski-Kubilius & Calvert, 2016). When students are taught to be aware of how their emotions, thoughts, and beliefs about their abilities influence their own behaviors and pursuit of excellence, they can be empowered to channel their energies toward their passions for learning. Bar-On's (1997) five competencies of emotional intelligence provide a framework for many of the skills taught within this curriculum (as cited in Bar-On, Maree, & Elias, 2007):

1. The ability to be aware of, to understand, and to express our emotions and feelings non-destructively.
2. The ability to understand how others feel and use this information to relate to them.

3. The ability to manage and control emotions so they work for us and not against us.
4. The ability to manage change, and to adapt and solve problems of a personal and interpersonal nature.
5. The ability to generate positive affect and be self-motivated. (p. 77)

Guided by Psychological Science and Research

The American Psychological Association (APA, 2015) documented 20 principles from psychological science that impact Pre-K–12 education. The principles in the areas of thinking and learning, motivation, social skills, classroom management, and assessment—many of which are incorporated within this curriculum—evidence the connections between psychological science and educational practice. APA added additional guidance specific to gifted learners in 2017, noting some of the most salient topics for this population, including growth mindset, assessing readiness, deliberate practice, and fostering talent development.

The evidence-based practices used in this curriculum have demonstrated effectiveness with gifted students in particular. Some of these lessons are derived from the first author's development of affective curriculum that specifically addressed perfectionism and coping, which demonstrated positive effects for decreasing components of unhealthy perfectionism (Mofield, 2008). We then expanded this focus to incorporate broader aspects of achievement motivation theories based on our collaborative efforts in studying the relationships of mindsets, achievement attitudes, coping, and perfectionism (Mofield & Parker Peters, 2015, 2018a, 2018b; Mofield, Parker Peters, & Chakraborti-Ghosh, 2016).

Organization

This text is divided into three sections that target specific topics and skills. Each lesson features an introduction section to provide background information regarding the psychosocial concepts addressed, including relevant research related to the idea and practical tips for cultivating the skills in the classroom (and beyond the lesson).

Part I: Persevering With Passion for Learning provides an introduction to the necessary ingredients for success. Students learn about the importance of cultivating interests as part of developing talent, specifically academic talent. Students also learn about the concepts of grit, deliberate practice, and how to find the optimal "flow" in pursuing challenges. Students think about the purpose in achieving excellence through understanding learning/mastery goals versus performance goals, and exploring a life philosophy. This section also includes strategies to develop tenacity, specifically by developing purposeful, meaningful goals, identifying the obstacles to achieving these goals, and developing a plan to move forward.

Part II: Growing Toward Excellence provides lessons to help students move beyond their comfort zones, take risks, and handle mistakes. Students learn about growth mindsets, unhealthy perfectionism versus pursuit of excellence, productive ways to handle mistakes and setbacks, reappraisals for interpreting stress, and the importance of risk-taking in learning.

Part III: Guiding Emotion Toward Excellence emphasizes social-emotional intelligence by guiding students to understand how their emotions influence behaviors, specifically their pursuit of excellence. Students develop self-awareness of their emotions and learn key strategies for managing impulses, anxiety, and/or fear. Students also learn the importance of testing assumptions of the mind, which affect relationships and how challenges and setbacks are interpreted. This section also provides opportunities for students to develop positive interpersonal skills and effective, assertive ways to communicate their emotions and work through conflicts.

Big Ideas

Each section focuses on specific big ideas (see Table 1). It is recommended that these big ideas are displayed so that students can make connections to their learning. In addition, students may develop other big idea statements that relate to the concepts presented.

Key Concepts

The curriculum promotes three major concepts throughout the lessons. These ideas can be emphasized and built upon as you continue to guide students' self-awareness and understanding.

Mindful excellence. We define this as being aware of how our thoughts, emotions, and beliefs about our own abilities influence our pursuit of excellence. When we are aware of the negative self-talk that we say to ourselves when confronted with a challenge, we are empowered to change our thinking. When we are aware of how

TABLE 1
Big Ideas

SECTION	BIG IDEAS
Part I: Persevering With a Passion for Learning Essential Question: What does it take to persevere?	Perseverance is rooted in purpose. To persevere is to channel enthusiasm into endurance.
Part II: Growing Toward Excellence Essential Question: How can I grow beyond the boundaries of my comfort zone?	Growth involves risk and courage. Growth can be uncomfortable.
Part III: Guiding Emotion Toward Excellence Essential Question: How can I manage emotions so they work for me, not against me?	Self-awareness leads to self-management. Self-awareness catalyzes change.

our emotions change in response to stressful situations, we are empowered to regulate those emotions. When we are aware that our abilities are changeable, we are empowered to change them. We refer to a pursuit of excellence as any endeavor toward achievement. A pursuit of excellence is different than a pursuit of perfection. A pursuit of excellence involves striving from the motivation for success rather than a motivation out of a fear of failure. Remind students to be mindful of their motivations behind their thoughts, emotions, and beliefs about their abilities. This awareness of how they pursue excellence can be the tool for managing the obstacles (such as fear of failure, lack of motivation, self-doubt, etc.) that often stand in the way of reaching goals.

Lean in and push through. This refers to being aware of any unpleasant emotion that is experienced (due to a challenge, conflict, or obstacle) and learning to push through the temporary discomfort. This phrase can be used to help students be aware that they are getting out of their comfort zone in learning or tackling a new challenge. By leaning into the struggle, the students can reframe the struggle as opportunity. This is part of developing emotional intelligence, as students become aware of an emotion and deal with it, rather than shoving it aside where the emotion may eventually resurface in other behaviors (e.g., lashing out in an argument, passive-aggressive behaviors, avoidance of new experiences and risk-taking in learning, etc.). "Lean in and push through" requires courage to step into unknown territory (e.g., push through the awkwardness of handling a conflict, feeling that others will not think you are smart if you fail, etc.). The phrase "lean in and push through" can be used to help students be aware of why they are feeling the emotion. What is the emotion motivating them to do? Is the challenge a true threat, or is it an opportunity to grow and move forward? Pushing through the discomfort will involve stretching, but these small steps of stretching enable growth.

Reframing thinking. This refers to techniques for teaching students how to adjust their perception of a situation or challenge. Many of the concepts in this curriculum (challenge, growth mindset, emotional intelligence, stress) relate directly to perception. As we researched each idea, we noticed a major pattern from all facets of psychological science—our thoughts can be reappraised or reframed. For example, do you perceive that intelligence is fixed? When this thought is reframed (i.e., intelligence is malleable), it affects how we pursue challenges. Do you perceive that you have control over your success and failures? If you feel that you can respond proactively to change your behaviors in response to your circumstances, this can lead to positive outcomes. Do you believe that stress is debilitating? If stress is perceived as enhancing, this can lead to better performance. As you teach these lessons, help students understand that reframing our thinking affects our emotions and beliefs, which affect our behaviors and relationships.

Figure 1 shows an overall model for considering obstacles within and out of our control, testing thoughts and assumptions, and regulating emotion. Over the course of the curriculum, students have opportunities to apply all of the strategies. Some lessons may emphasize a row or a column. For example, students learn to think through the context of a situation (moving left to right), and learn to ask what is in their control and what is not within their control (Lesson 7 and Lesson 14). From here, they learn to take the next step (moving down the last row), which can often build positive emotion for moving forward. Other lessons may emphasize the emotional-thought connections, building on the idea of self-awareness. Students are led through the first column. What is the situation, and what did you think of that situation? (How did you interpret it? What emotion is linked with this thought?) From here, students can learn to logically dispute the thought or assumption (Lessons 12 and 20), or learn strategies to regulate the emotion through coping strategies (Lessons 15 and 19).

What Drives Excellence?

The curriculum is meant to provide lesson ideas and activities to develop a drive for excellence. Table 2 is an overview of the obstacles and concepts (fuel) for gearing up for a successful drive toward excellence. As you complete selected lessons, you may post a chart, adding concepts as various lessons are completed.

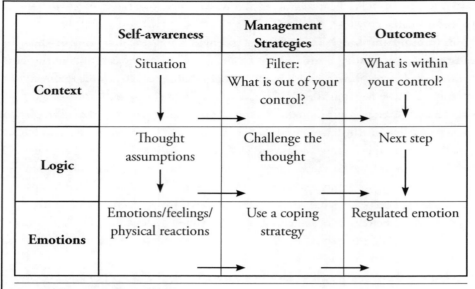

	Self-awareness	Management Strategies	Outcomes
Context	Situation	Filter: What is out of your control?	What is within your control?
Logic	Thought assumptions	Challenge the thought	Next step
Emotions	Emotions/feelings/ physical reactions	Use a coping strategy	Regulated emotion

FIGURE 1. Reframing thinking model.

Lesson Components

Each lesson includes lesson objectives that delineate what students should know, do, and/or understand as a result of the lesson. Materials outline specific handouts, links to videos, or other hands-on materials needed to facilitate the lesson. An Introduction section provides a hook. This is followed by Class Activities that engage students to think, respond, and interact with the concept. Because we know that teachers need to justify instructional time by tying in social-emotional learning with content, we offer Curriculum Extensions, which serve as suggestions for embedding literature, informational texts, and writing in response to the ideas in a lesson. The Personal Reflections are opportunities for students to respond to ideas in a personal journal (which need not be shared or collected by the teacher). The Conclusion Connections offer ways to connect students to how the lesson relates to ideas in other lessons, how the lesson relates to big idea statements (see Table 1), and/or how the lesson relates to mindful excellence, lean in and push through, or reframing thinking. They serve as a way to help the student see the skill as one of many factors that drive achievement motivation. Finally, Checks for Understanding offer ideas for exit tickets or quick ways to use formative assessment to determine how well students understand the lesson concepts.

TABLE 2

Obstacles and Fuel for a Drive for Excellence

	OBSTACLES TO MINDFUL EXCELLENCE	FUEL FOR MINDFUL EXCELLENCE
Lesson 4	Performance goals	Learning/mastery goals
Lesson 7	Lack of self-control—feels pleasant to give in to gratification	Applied use of self-control (emotions—understanding the unpleasant emotion of delayed gratification—must go through the pain of discomfort)
Lesson 10	Fixed mindset	Growth mindset
Lesson 11	Unhealthy perfectionism	Healthy perfectionism (pursuit of excellence)
Lesson 14	Not feeling that you have control	Feeling that you have control
Lesson 15	Avoidance coping	Approach coping
Lesson 16	Perceiving stress as debilitating	Perceiving stress as enhancing
Lesson 17	Procrastinating	Prioritizing
Lesson 18	Avoiding feelings of discomfort—reverting to numbing of feelings	Leaning into discomfort
Lesson 19	Unaware of how emotions impact self and behaviors	Self-aware of how emotions affect self and behaviors
Lesson 20	Pessimism (nothing can change—failure is permanent)	Optimism (failure is temporary)
Lessons 22–23	Assumptions control behaviors	Assumptions are tested before developing conclusions
Lesson 24	Passive or aggressive behaviors	Assertive behaviors

Tips for Using This Curriculum

Although the lessons were sequenced purposefully, you may wish to teach only some lessons or even parts of lessons. We recommend you teach lessons that are most pertinent to the group you are teaching. For example, you may not need to address the issue of perfectionism with your students. Perhaps you need to spend more time on the lesson about procrastination. You know your students best. Follow their interests and learning. You may also find that some lessons are more appropriate for a small group of students, and we recommend small-group instruction or use of stations when this need arises. It is also important to establish a community of learners in which you build trust in a context where students feel comfortable sharing their motivations, emotions, or fears. Finally, it is important to note that some students may have social-emotional issues that need professional attention. This curriculum is not meant to serve as a tool for therapy. It is meant to help educators help students become self-aware of their thoughts, emotions, and beliefs, especially as they relate to pursuing excellence.

Use With Gifted Students

Many gifted education programs seek the use of special social-emotional curriculum to address many of the issues within this curriculum (identifying student interests, dealing with perfectionism, handling mistakes, managing emotional intensities). These lessons address many needs related to giftedness, and we also created a supplemental guide (available on the book's webpage at https://www.prufrock.com/teaching-tenacity-resources.aspx) that can be used to help gifted students become aware of how their exceptional abilities affect their thoughts, emotions, and beliefs about their abilities. The webpage also includes a Gifted Extended Reflections section, which provides questions, activities, and additional ideas for relating giftedness to many of the lessons. Activities also align well with the National Association for Gifted Children Gifted Programming Standards for Grades K–12, specifically self-understanding (e.g., educators assist students with gifts and talents in developing identities supportive of achievement), awareness of needs (educators provide role models for students with gifts and talents that match their abilities and interests), and cognitive and affective growth (a standards chart is included at the end of the book).

Benefits for Disadvantaged Populations

Many students arrive at school without some of the traits or experiences that propel student success. Instead of purposeful afterschool or summertime enrichment, these students may be consumed with helping a family member, working to support loved ones, or left to their own devices. Although these students may not be intentionally kept from experiences that could support progress, their personal circumstances prevent it. These lessons support the development of untapped and unidentified potential by providing explicit guidance on developing emotional regulation, assertive communication skills, and goal-oriented behaviors. As noted in a national report shining a light on the achievement—or lack of achievement—among low-income, high-ability learners, the percentage of American school children who live in poverty is only increasing; thus, it is all the more important to support a psychological identity of high achievement among this group (Olszewski-Kubilius & Clarenbach, 2012). Expectations for this group should not be lowered. These lessons support the development of specific psychosocial variables that will aid this group of students as they combat the challenges related to stereotype threat, motivation, lack of supports for organization, or other factors that may hinder achievement.

Guiding Underachievers

This curriculum is a guide to help students achieve. Underachievement, when students achieve significantly below their potential, is often due to a lack of motivation or perceived support (see Siegle & McCoach, 2005). Many ideas and lessons in this curriculum can be used to address motivational issues with underachievers. For example, Lessons 7, 12, 15, 17, 18, and 19 can be used to teach self-regulation skills. See the book's webpage (https://www.prufrock.com/teaching-tenacity-resources.aspx) for a list of more lesson connections related to underachievement.

Diving In

Overall, this text assists educators as they cultivate the nonacademic skills necessary to catalyze student success. Although students have many talents and abilities that set the stage for future achievement, psychosocial skills targeting perseverance, tenacity, and sustained effort provide the impetus that students need to overcome challenges and setbacks they might experience as they reach to achieve. It's time to dive in and unlock potential. As stated before, don't worry about teaching every lesson, or even all components of a lesson. Do what is relevant and meaningful for your students. Follow their voices, and empower their talents!

Pre- and Postassessment

The pre- and postassessment handout includes questions to measure students' growth in understanding positive approaches to persevere, handle setbacks, and deal with unpleasant emotion. A rubric is provided to determine growth in student responses. We do not recommend that such assessments be graded, rather that they be used to document personal growth and understanding about social-emotional learning. The rubric may also be used to understand how specific social-emotional-motivational strategies are applied to the questions.

Additionally, the self-assessment handout can help students identify their strengths and weaknesses related to lesson concepts. Refer to the charts at the beginning of each section that show the specific social-emotional concepts addressed within the lessons. These may be useful as you plan to address the most relevant needs among your students.

Pre- and Postassessment

Directions: Answer the following questions based on your understanding of the role of thoughts, emotions, and beliefs as they relate to the pursuit of excellence.

1. Identify at least five factors that are important for success. How are they related?

2. Imagine a personal goal. Explain how you would stick to achieving your goal.

Name:_____ Date: _____

Pre- and Postassessment, *continued*

3. Imagine you feel stressed out before a test. Explain how you would mentally prepare to do your best.

4. What advice would you give a friend who wants to quit at something because he feels he's not very good at it right away?

5. How does being aware of our emotions help us manage emotions?

Rubric for Pre- and Postassessment

Name: _____ Date: _____

QUESTION	1	2	3	4
1	Incomplete response reflects inaccurate understanding.	Response lacks understanding.	Includes less than five concepts or includes some repeated concepts. Relationships are not clear.	Includes concepts related to opportunity, motivation, passion/interests, growth mindset, perseverance (grit, tenacity, task-commitment, self-control), creativity. Shows how one factor influences another (we are motivated by our interests, etc.)
2	Incomplete response reflects inaccurate understanding.	A strategy is mentioned, but it is not linked to purpose, envisioning obstacles, establishing plans, or pursuing improvement through deliberate practice or flow.	Includes only a few elements of WOOP (visualizing goal, thinking through obstacles). Mentions only one strategy.	Includes a personal goal with at least two strategies listed: all elements of WOOP wish-outcome-obstacle-plan, reference to purpose/learning goal/why, striving for flow, planning for deliberate practice, taking small STEPs, etc.
3	Incomplete response reflects inaccurate understanding.	Response does not adequately demonstrate an understanding of how stress can be reframed or regulated to help prepare for a challenge. Student may refer to avoidance coping.	One to two strategies are mentioned, but it is not clear that the strategies promote self-awareness of approach-coping (problem solving or seeking social support) or reframing stress.	Response includes at least two of the following: being aware that physical reaction prepares for a challenge, reframing the stress as excitement (I'm excited, I'm excited, I'm excited), taking time to regulate stress (walk, deep breaths, mindfulness, etc.), using approach coping (problem solving, seeking social support).
4	Incomplete response reflects inaccurate understanding	Response does not reflect an adequate understanding of how to persevere through difficulty with growth mindset beliefs.	Advice is merely encouragement—there is just a vague reference to growth mindset beliefs.	Advice refers to at least two concepts: growth mindset (intelligence can grow), effort leads to growth, and mistakes help us grow. Response may include advice for action (seeking support), or advice for unpleasant emotion—lean in and push through.

Rubric for Pre- and Postassessment, *continued*

QUESTION	1	2	3	4
5	Incomplete response reflects inaccurate understanding.	Response does not reflect adequate understanding of how emotions help us become self-aware of our needs and motives, which helps one be aware of how to respond to situations.	Response only refers to how to manage emotion or only refers to self-awareness. No clear connection is made.	Response includes a reference to understanding the purpose of emotion and how awareness helps us change our impulse reactions. Understanding emotions help us express them appropriately. Response includes the awareness of how emotions affect behaviors, relationships, and pursuit of excellence.

Self-Assessment of Social-Emotional Strengths

Directions: Complete the chart. Note how strongly you agree or disagree with each statement.

	CONCEPT	STRONGLY DISAGREE	DISAGREE	SOMETIMES	AGREE	STRONGLY AGREE
I am usually satisfied with my work and feel proud of what I do.	Self-regard					
I am usually aware of my emotions as they relate to pursuing a challenge. (I know if I am feeling disinterest, anxiety, fear, excitement, etc.)	Emotional self-awareness					
I am usually aware of what is causing me to feel a certain way.	Emotional self-awareness					
I can usually tell how others are feeling.	Empathy					
I feel confident in speaking up for myself.	Assertiveness					
When I make a goal, I am usually able to stick to it.	Academic perseverance/ self-motivation					
I feel comfortable telling others how I feel, even if I am feeling upset, angry, or afraid.	Assertiveness					
I am usually able to manage my stress when I'm stressed out.	Stress tolerance					
I generally feel I can make things happen. I have a sense of control when thinking about my future.	Independence/ optimism/hope					
I can work well with others in group situations.	Social responsibility/ interpersonal relationships					

Self-Assessment of Social-Emotional Strengths, *continued*

CONCEPT		STRONGLY DISAGREE	DISAGREE	SOMETIMES	AGREE	STRONGLY AGREE
I feel at ease and comfortable being with others, especially my friends.	Interpersonal relationships					
I am usually able to control intense emotions (not burst out, not show irresponsible behavior).	Impulse control					
I think I can change my intelligence.	Self-regard/independence					
I can test my inner thoughts against the reality of the situation (I can tell if what I'm thinking is really true).	Reality-testing					
When I encounter an obstacle, I can usually problem solve through it fairly quickly.	Problem solving					
When I set a personal goal, I will usually enthusiastically commit to achieving it.	Self-actualization/academic perseverance/self-motivation					
When I encounter a setback, I can usually move forward with a positive and hopeful outlook.	Optimism					
I enjoy working hard to improve my performance, especially on things I am interested in.	Self-actualization/academic perseverance/self-motivation					
When I encounter something new, I can usually adjust well, even through the new difficulties.	Flexibility/adaptability					
I have self-respect and like who I am.	Self-regard					

Note. Concepts are from Bar-On's (1997) factors of emotional intelligence.

PART I

Persevering With a Passion for Learning

Essential Question

What does it take to persevere?

Big Ideas

- Perseverance is rooted in purpose.
- To persevere is to channel enthusiasm into endurance.

Lesson Outline

LESSON	KEY QUESTION	CONCEPTS
Lesson 1: Ingredients for Success	What factors are necessary to develop one's potential?	Academic mindset
Lesson 2: Talent Meets Passion	What's interesting to me?	Self-awareness, discovering interests
Lesson 3: Encounters With Eminent Individuals	How do eminent individuals maximize their heights of potential?	Understanding talent development
Lesson 4: The Why Factor	How can I be motivated to pursue excellence?	Self-awareness, self-motivation

LESSON	KEY QUESTION	CONCEPTS
Lesson 5: Tenacity	How can I stick to my goals?	Self-motivation
Lesson 6: Grit	What does it mean to be gritty?	Academic perseverance, self-motivation
Lesson 7: Face-to-Face With Obstacles	What's holding me back?	Academic perseverance, self-motivation
Lesson 8: Deliberate Practice	Does practice make perfect?	Academic perseverance, self-motivation
Lesson 9: Getting in the Flow	What is the relationship between work and happiness?	Self-actualization

Part I introduces motivational factors leading to success. Talent alone does not guarantee achievement or success. Ability does not guarantee future triumphs. Achievement is the coalescence of multiple factors—ability, opportunity, motivation, etc. All students at all levels have the capacity to improve. In the first few lessons, students explore the development of a passion for learning. In the second half of Part I, the lessons introduce strategies to tackle obstacles, develop grit, and build tenacity toward meeting set goals. Part I is also driven by one of Bar-On's (1997) major competencies for emotional intelligence, the ability to generate positive affect to be self-motivated (as cited in Bar-On, Maree, & Elias, 2007). This section provides a broad look at the psychosocial concepts that will drive further self-understanding in later lessons. As you teach Part I, remind students of the big ideas. You may write these ideas on a poster and refer to them during discussion as you facilitate the lessons.

Ingredients for Success

Specific factors support optimal development, including ability, task commitment, interest, passion, opportunity, motivation, creativity, and growth mindset (Subotnik et al., 2011). These ingredients help grow ability to unknown heights of potential:

1. **Task commitment:** The defining qualities of task commitment include perseverance, endurance, hard work, dedicated practice, self-confidence, and belief in self (Renzulli, 1986).

2. **Interest and passion:** These factors play a role in transforming ability into its greatest form. When students discover their interests and passions for learning, they can move toward high achievement in the "interest" domain.

3. **Perseverance:** Duckworth (2016) noted, "enthusiasm is common, endurance is rare" (p. 56). It is one thing for students to want to start a task or project, but following through to completion requires perseverance. Persevering is rooted in purpose and is maintained with motivation and a plan to work through obstacles.

4. **Opportunity:** Without opportunities to develop talent, it will not flourish. Without opportunities to work through challenges, task commitment and perseverance will not be strengthened. Access to opportunity matters. These opportunities may include access to high-level classes, resources, or even opportunities to step out of one's comfort zone. When opportunities are presented, we must encourage students to take these opportunities.

5. **Motivation:** According to Deci and Ryan (2008), motivation, or self-determination to move forward or complete a task, stems from internal needs, including competence ("I think I can!") and autonomy ("I have some control!"). If we want students to be motivated toward a task or skill, they must feel that they are capable of experiencing success and feel that they have some

23

control in their success. These two factors are critical in cultivating intrinsic motivation.

6. **Creativity:** Creativity allows for flexibility, originality, and fluidity of thinking (Torrance, 1974). We should prepare students to be creative producers in their area of interest (and eventually area of expertise). The hallmark of high achievement is creative production in a field, such as contributing new ideas that help solve problems in our world.

7. **Growth mindset:** What you believe about your intelligence can greatly affect how and to what extent you achieve. This is popularly known as *mindset*. Do students believe that their abilities have been and will remain stable, or do they believe that abilities are a starting point for further development? Dweck (2006) showed that growth mindset is the catalyst that helps other ingredients, including ability, grow. When students believe that they can get smarter (in a given domain), motivation to persevere will likely follow. When a student believes that mistakes are opportunities for learning, a student is much more likely to explore creativity. (See Part II for more discussion on growth mindset.)

This lesson provides an opportunity for introspective reflection, allowing students to consider how these factors are influential in supporting their continued success.

Big Idea

What factors are necessary to develop one's potential?

Objectives

Students will:

- differentiate between potential and achievement,
- analyze the cause-effect relationships between the factors necessary for developing potential, and
- read "If" and analyze the poem's meaning by relating it to the factors studied.

Materials

- Clear glass or plastic cup
- Baking soda (about 1–2 tablespoons)
- 1/3-cup of vinegar
- Bottle of water
- "If" by Rudyard Kipling (available online)

Introduction

Ask students: *How do you define success? Can you be successful without being talented? Can you be talented without being successful? What is the difference between potential and achievement? Do they mean the same thing?* In this lesson, students will continue to explore these questions.

Class Activities

1. Display a clear glass or plastic cup with about 1/3-cup of vinegar already in it. Explain that potential is like the cup: *It is not completely full, but is capable of holding whatever is put there. Ability is like the clear liquid already in the cup. It is one of many ingredients that counts for "meeting one's potential." It looks like ability is not enough for someone to reach his or her potential. What else do you think is needed?* List student responses on the board. As you work with the list, categorize them with student input. Lead students to articulate these factors: task commitment, interest/passion, perseverance, opportunities, motivation, and creativity. List them on the board.

2. Discuss each factor as you pour a bit of water, filling the cup only about 3/4 full. (*Note.* There are other factors essential for success. The ones in this lesson will be the focus of the unit, as they are explicitly discussed within talent development [Subotnik et al., 2011].)

3. Explain that there is one more important ingredient that actually "grows" these other factors, including ability. This last ingredient also interacts with the other factors to help one develop (or "reach") his or her fullest potential. Ask: *What do you think it is?*

4. Pour about one tablespoon of baking soda into the cup. You may need to be close to a trashcan. The combined factors bubble over, reaching heights above defined potential. Explain: *The baking soda represents one's belief in his or her abilities (growth mindset). When you believe that abilities can grow, you are motivated to take on challenging experiences to grow further. You seek opportunities that will develop abilities and talents further; you see effort, hard work, or perseverance as essential to stretch your abilities further; and you are more likely to be intrinsically motivated to pursue passions and interests without fear of failure. You pursue high levels of achievement, not to prove your worth or value, but because of the drive to learn, improve, and challenge yourself to do something purposeful. As a result of cultivating a strong interest and passion, you are free to*

create. Creativity in this sense means to produce something new for the world, to develop a new idea, to add to one's field of study.

5. Ask students:

   ■ *Is the cup the best metaphor for potential? Why or why not? Was it big enough to hold all of the ingredients?* (Guide students to understand that a person's true potential is unknown [see Dweck 2000, 2006]. We are not able to accurately measure a person's future potential, only a person's current ability. We really do not know how big the cup is. Even potential is expandable. Perhaps a better metaphor is an expandable cup.)

   ■ *Because potential is unknowable, how does this influence how we view the other ingredients?* (The more we add perseverance, the more we add motivation, the more we add passion, etc., the more likely we can achieve the potential. The good news is these factors are controllable.)

   ■ *What might be a better metaphor for potential?* (Consider a seed; we don't know how big the tree can grow, but we can do everything we can to help it grow. The potential of the tree can be maximized when fertilizer is added.)

   ■ *According to Daniel Coyle, "Talent is not a possession, it's a construction project" (as cited in Fogarty, Kerns, & Pete, 2018). Do you agree or disagree? Based on this lesson, how can you create your own metaphor for how talent is constructed?*

Conclusion Connections

Introduce the term *mindful excellence*. Ask: *What do these terms (mindful and excellence) mean in isolation? What might they mean together?* (Mindful simply means to be aware or conscious of something; excellence is the quality of being outstanding.) Tell students: *As we continue to learn about the qualities of success, we will refer to mindful excellence as being aware of how our thoughts, emotions, and beliefs about abilities affect how we pursue developing our own unknowable potential. Mindful excellence is about being aware of these factors and how they affect our behaviors, relationships, and pursuit of excellence.*

Curriculum Extension

Using the poem "If" by Rudyard Kipling, lead a Socratic Seminar or whole-class discussion.

- Which "If" statement is the most important? Why?
- What paradoxes do you notice in the poem? (A paradox is two seemingly different ideas existing at the same time, such as triumph and disaster.)
- Which ingredients essential for achieving potential are illuminated in the poem? (Remind students of the factors: perseverance, passion, motivation, and growth mindset.)
- How is the idea of mindful excellence evident in the poem?

Then, have students write their own "If" poem with at least four "If" statements based on what they know about the ingredients for success, ending the poem with "then you will reach ever greater heights."

Personal Reflection

Have students respond to the following: *Which "ingredient for success" is easiest for you to apply? How has this lesson made you think about these "ingredients" differently? By applying mindful excellence, what are your attitudes about some of these factors, and how might these attitudes affect the other ingredients?*

Check for Understanding

Display the words *opportunity, perseverance, motivation, passion, growth mindset,* and *creativity*. Ask students to write these words on a sheet of paper and draw arrows between them with explanations to show how they relate to one another.

Talent Meets Passion

Where does enthusiasm come from? It starts with a budding interest. If we want to promote intrinsic motivation among students, we must first help students discover their interests and facilitate the development of these interests.

Two basic types of interests can be observed in students: situational and individual. *Situational interests* tend to be temporary; they are not the interests that carry passion to fuel a lifetime study of a topic. Instead, situational interests may manifest as a result of an interesting discussion in class about World War II that leads to some Internet searches to learn more about the topic. *Individual interests* are much deeper; they create deep roots and are stable over time without outside reward or support, and situational interests can become individual interests (Hidi & Renninger, 2006). For example, the student who followed up class discussion with Internet searches about World War II may be captivated by the behaviors exhibited by people during that time in history. Or a student may realize an interest in psychology to learn more about why people behave in a particular way. Beyond Internet searches, this student reads about psychology and may seek courses or independent study, find expert-mentors, or even pursue a major in psychology. Externally, the student would not be rewarded for any of these behaviors, but the student would be intrinsically fueled by continually learning more about the target of his passion for learning. Although we want students to find and foster their individual interests, it may be just as important for them to first develop situational interests that will later mature into more stable, passion-driven individual interests.

Exposure matters in interest development. If Michael Phelps had never been taken to a pool as a child, would he be the Olympian he is today? It is important for students to try different interests and see what fits. An evening at the observatory could fuel further interest in astronomy and lead to further reading, independent research, creative thinking, or even future relationships with others who share their interest.

Further, if exposure is critical to the development of interests that lead to talent development, then we must also consider access. Although we cannot provide access to all resources and interest areas to reach all students, education can provide the first glance at or opportunity to experience an unknown interest. The first moments of exposure are critical and set the stage for developing a passion for learning. Educators matter in interest and academic talent development, especially for students who may experience many life moments vicariously through the examples and stories shared in the classroom. Without the opportunities and enrichment you provide, our next scholars may not even realize that an interest exists.

Providing such opportunities to nurture burgeoning interests can produce what Ericsson and Pool (2016) described as the "bent-twig" effect. One small opportunity for growth early on can change a child's entire direction and talent trajectory. In lesson planning, offering students choices can be a way to broaden horizons and expose students to new areas of interest. This may include opportunities to explore tangential interests related to the content studied. You can also nudge them further with encouragement and acknowledgement of their budding potential and show them how they can pursue and apply their talents.

This lesson is aimed at exposing students to interests that they may not even know they have. Allow them the joy of browsing and stumbling upon a seed that just might be a starting point for a lifetime of learning.

Big Idea

What's interesting to me?

Objectives

Students will:
- be able to identify potential discipline-specific interests, and
- understand that talent comes to fruition when an interest is deepened and developed.

Materials

- Handout 2.1: Exploring Academic Interests
- Student access to "The Great Courses" website (available at https://www.thegreatcourses.com) or university online course catalogs

■ (Optional) Video: "Stop Searching for Your Passion" by Terri Trespicio (last 3 minutes; available at https://www.youtube.com/watch?v=6MBaFL7sCb8)

Introduction

1. Divide students into groups of three. Ask students to list as many careers as they can think of (at least 25). Encourage students to go beyond broad careers, such as "medical doctor." Guide them to think of "fields of study" and consider specific careers within these fields (types of medicine, engineering, etc.).

2. After they compile their lists, ask students to sort the careers into three or four groups (one group cannot be "other"). Ask: *How would you label these categories?*

3. After students share their categories, ask them to reorganize. Ask: *What's another way of organizing these? What are your new category names? What do all careers have in common?* (They involve contributing to society, they involve people spending a large portion of their lives preparing for the career and growing in the career, etc.)

4. Ask: *How would you define "career"? How would you define "vocation"? How is a career different than a job?* Explain that *career* is defined as "an occupation undertaken for a significant period of a person's life and with opportunities for progress." A *vocation* is "a particular occupation, business, or profession; calling; a strong impulse or inclination to follow a particular activity or career." Because careers involve a significant period of a person's life, they should be of high interest. Note that vocation implies a connotation to help others in society. The goal involves contributing to positive change in the world.

Class Activities

1. Ask: *If you could learn more about anything in the world, what would you want to learn about?* Elicit responses. Explain that this gives insight into "interest," a critical component in developing potential. To become accomplished in a field of study, one must have a deep interest in the content. This often comes from being exposed to an interest at an early age. Explain that there are many fields and subfields of study that many people don't even know exist.

2. Ask students to explore courses on The Great Courses website (or a university course online catalog). Allow them 5–10 minutes to simply browse and read about courses and fields.

3. Distribute Handout 2.1: Exploring Academic Interests for students to complete. Allow students to share their responses.

4. Ask: *Does passion lead to success, or does success lead to passion?* Discuss caveats related to "finding your passion." Sometimes this idea can be overwhelming for students, especially at an age where they are still being exposed to content areas to develop their interests. Interests can likely turn into passions, but it is often the successful experiences in our lives that lead to the development of passions.

5. (Optional) Show the video "Stop Searching for Your Passion" by Terri Trespicio—especially the last 3 minutes. A passion "for learning" versus a "passion" may be a more relevant concept at this age. As students learn about their interests through learning and exploration, a passion can develop.

Conclusion Connections

Remind students of mindful excellence. Ask: *How does understanding your interests relate to your pursuit of excellence?*

Curriculum Extension

Ask students to choose one course description from The Great Courses (or university online course catalog). Encourage them to research more information on their own regarding the topic, based on inspiration from this lesson. Ask students to explore the purpose of the field related to their topic, the problems addressed within the field, and the types of information used in the field to make decisions. Ask: *How does this field help society?*

Personal Reflection

Have students respond to the following: *What fields of study relate to your interests? How does interest influence the other elements studied in the cup illustration (from Lesson*

1)? Explain how interest relates to at least two of the following: motivation, perseverance, creativity, or opportunity.

Check for Understanding

Have students complete an exit ticket: *Explain how interest is like _____ (choose from one of the following: a ring, glue, sugar, or bricks). How does interest relate to emotion? Why is this important to long-term pursuits of excellence?*

Name: _____ Date: _____

Exploring Academic Interests

Directions: After looking over various course descriptions on selected websites, list 10 courses you find interesting. They do not have to be within the same field of study. You are welcome to explore various topics and fields.

1. _____   6. _____

2. _____   7. _____

3. _____   8. _____

4. _____   9. _____

5. _____   10. _____

Answer the following questions.

1. What pattern do you notice about the courses you listed?

2. How do these courses relate to potential career interests? What fields of study do your interests cover?

3. In what ways might you explore an interesting topic further (without necessarily purchasing the course)? Does this ignite a desire for you to learn information on your own? If so, what would be a good next step?

Encounters With Eminent Individuals

n this lesson, students explore individuals who have made it; the ingredients for success (task commitment, interest, passion, perseverance, motivation, creativity, opportunity, and growth mindset) combined in a way that led to their achievement. Each individual found a passion that has transformed into a lasting legacy based upon actualized performance or production. As we note for students, success rarely just happens.

Bloom (1985) and colleagues followed 120 eminent individuals, including musicians, athletes, and scientists, finding patterns among their lifepaths, regardless of their craft. Although many began activities, such as music lessons or swimming, as a result of a parent's decision, they stayed with the activities out of their own volition. In the early years with a craft, enjoyment rather than skill development is primary. Students explore and ultimately determine whether the activity is going to develop into more than an afterschool hobby. Parents, coaches, and instructors highlight the fun and enjoyment before emphasizing the dedication and commitment necessary to proceed. This is the Romance stage of talent development (Whitehead, 1929) in which students enjoy freedom and discovery, where interests can be awakened and aroused, but skill refinement is not yet the target. We watch for and encourage students to continue with the craft because they enjoy it; they are drawn to it, not because it is required or because it will create a future career. We watch for the students' sustained effort, exerted without prodding, which may signal that the interest is developing into one that is valued and may last for more than a season.

For interest to bloom into a lifelong passion, the interest must be more than situational. Duckworth (2016) noted that parents and teachers can set the stage for further development by providing a high level of support and maintaining high expectations. By doing so, a student's potential can become excellence. Once a student finds an area of interest and begins to develop to higher levels, goals may change for both the student and her supporters. Now that the student has found a craft that can develop with passion and perseverance, expectations might change. The student no longer expects to simply participate in writing activities because they are fun and she does well; she expects to be published. The student looks to those who are known in her field of interest; she looks to famous journalists, poets, or novelists, admiring their work and desiring to rise to their level of eminence.

There are eminent individuals in all professions—those who have reached an exceptional high performance level or have produced creative contributions within their field. Marie Curie, Simone Biles, and Isaac Newton could be considered eminent. Newton is known for his expertise in mathematics and physics in addition to his theory of gravity. Biles is known for her athletic prowess and has been called the "greatest gymnast of all time," winning several Olympic gold medals. Curie is known for her expertise in chemistry and physics, winning coveted Nobel Prizes in both areas. They climbed to the top of their fields and are known for expertise and production.

During this lesson, remind students of the big ideas for Part I. Somewhere along the journey toward eminence, the high-level performer realizes "I want to do this, I can do this, I will do this, and I'm doing what I dreamed of doing" (Fogarty et al., 2018). Guide students to understand the thinking behind such pursuits and explore these ideas as they can relate to student lives.

Big Idea

How do eminent individuals maximize their heights of potential?

Objectives

Students will be able to examine the stages of the talent development process.

Materials

- Handout 3.1: Eminent Investigation
- A few dominoes (to show how opportunity leads to more opportunity)
- Student access to research an eminent person (Internet, biography books, etc.)

Introduction

1. Ask students to work in small groups to list individuals who have reached exceptional levels of achievement. These individuals are likely famous for their significant contributions to their fields (e.g., Marie Curie, Galileo, Steve Jobs, Thomas Edison, Hans Christian Andersen, J. K. Rowling, etc.) or for their exceptional performances (in music, sports, etc.). If needed, provide additional hints to students by asking them to think in categories (e.g., science, Olympics, literature, etc.).

2. Ask students to develop broad big idea statements about these individuals. If students need additional support, they may use one or more of these words in their big idea statement: *deliberate, commitment, persistence, talent, ability, creativity, innovation, accomplished* (e.g., "These accomplished individuals have made creative contributions to society").

Class Activities

1. Explain that each individual did not just end up "eminent" by luck. Such individuals develop their talents over time. Explain the stages of the talent development process (Bloom, 1985):
   - **Romance stage: Developing an interest.** An individual is given opportunities to explore and play, developing a deep interest in a given field. This can happen at very early ages or even later (in middle school or high school) as students are exposed to more opportunities.
   - **Precision stage: Honing the skill further.** The individual sharpens his skills through systematic training (e.g., use of coach, good teacher, etc.).
   - **Integration stage: Developing mastery and expertise.** The individual studies with a master teacher, benefitting from a mentor who helps him develop expertise or even eminence (exceptional productive achievement) in a field.

2. Explain that for individuals to reach these heights of success, they needed more than high ability, perseverance, and motivation. They had to have *opportunities* to work really hard on developing these abilities. Sometimes these opportunities came by chance or luck, and sometimes they were pursued. For example, as a teenager, Bill Gates attended a school that happened to have a computer club. The school was given a giant computer; Gates spent excessive amounts of time learning how to program using the giant computer.

Then, it so happened that he lived only a few miles away from a university that had a super-computer, where he continued to spend hours of his free time programming. Each opportunity led to the next one. Demonstrate this with dominoes. Each domino represents an opportunity. As one opportunity is taken (one domino falling), it opens the door for another opportunity (another domino falling), and another (another domino falling).

3. Distribute Handout 3.1: Eminent Investigation. Ask students to research the life of an eminent individual (preferably self-selected). This may be from a biography study or through Internet research. In subsequent lessons, students may revisit their investigations to explore how their individuals displayed other skills (grit, tenacity, deliberate practice, etc.).

4. Students should share findings with a partner or in small groups. Consider asking students to complete a creative visual, such as an infographic, Prezi, Glogster, etc., to present their findings. Guide students to discover patterns for "How did the individuals make a major commitment to being the best they can be?"

Conclusion Connections

Remind students of mindful excellence. Ask: *How does learning about an eminent individual's life help us develop mindful excellence? How does the big idea "To persevere is to channel enthusiasm into endurance" relate to your own personal pursuits and interests?*

Curriculum Extension

Beyond initial online research, have students read a biography or autobiography on the individual they are studying for Handout 3.1. Ask students to reflect: *How did the historical or social context influence the individual? How did the individual's goals change throughout his or her life, and why? What were the key beliefs, values, and motivations of the individual? How did other people and events influence the person's motivation?*

Personal Reflection

Have students respond to the following: *After learning about the eminent individual, how does this make you more self-aware of your own strengths and opportunities? What part of the eminent person's life was most inspiring and why?*

Check for Understanding

Assess student responses on Handout 3.1: Eminent Investigation.

Name:_____ Date:_____

Eminent Investigation

Directions: Research an eminent individual. Compile information about how the eminent person developed exceptional skills using your own paper or a computer. You may need to review several sources. You may not be able to complete all parts.

1. The individual I will research is _____ .

2. Provide a brief bullet point biography review about the person. Include basic information, such as when and where the person was born, what the person is known for, and the key contributions of the person.

3. **Stage 1: Development of interest.** When did this individual develop an interest in this field? What early opportunities was he or she provided to develop these interests (was it early in life or later?)? Were there elements of "luck" at play? How did one opportunity lead to another?

4. **Stage 2: Development of skill.** What kind of special training did this individual experience to sharpen his or her skills?

5. **Stage 3: Development of expertise and mastery.** How did the person develop exceptional skills and provide significant contribution? Who were the special mentors in the person's life at this stage?

6. What obstacles did this person encounter? In what ways did the person approach the obstacles? What did the person learn from these obstacles? In what ways did the individual display perseverance and task commitment?

7. What factors played a role in the person's motivation towards his or her goal? What was the reason he or she wanted to achieve at a high level? What kept the person motivated toward the goals, even through difficulty? (Consider sources of inspiration.)

The Why Factor

In this lesson, students will explore the "why" for pursuing excellence and reflect on what invigorates them to push through when work becomes tedious. At the heart of this is motivation—"the real constraint on expertise" (Barr, 2012, p. 7). The key to persevering is beyond just wanting to "be the best" or doing a hobby well; perseverance is rooted in purpose—the reasons for the dedication and satisfaction that come with continued progress in an area of interest.

Elliott and Harackiewicz (1996) explained two types of goals, mastery goals and performance goals. *Mastery goals* are sometimes called learning goals. When students set mastery goals, they are interested in learning more and mastering the craft for the sake of furthering personal knowledge or sharpening their skills. On the other hand, *performance goals* are goals motivated out of the goal to "look smart" (known as performance-approach goals) or to "avoid looking stupid" (known as performance-avoidance goals).

Consider perfectionistic students who are obsessed with getting straight A's. There may not be any deep-rooted interest in learning the content, only in earning A's to please others or prove self-worth. Individuals who set performance goals are more likely to worry, have anxiety, and adopt fixed mindset beliefs about intelligence. They are less likely to persevere through challenges and more likely to view challenges as threatening to their self-worth. These goals, however, can be reframed into mastery or learning goals, where the focus is on continuous learning and improvement over time.

Should we discourage students from setting goals to make good grades? Should we discourage students from setting goals to win competitions, etc.? No. Competition can actually be highly motivating. The etymology of competition means "strive in common." Striving with others provides the necessary "push" and motivation for the next step of improvement. Even among students with deep-rooted mastery goals, there may be opportunity for short-term performance goals to fuel long-term mastery goals. For example, a swimmer may have the goal of making an Olympic appearance; this, in the student's mind, would demonstrate that he has mastered swimming. In order to achieve this long-term mastery goal, the swimmer must also make smaller goals along the way. He sets goals of placing in regional and national meets over the course of several years to move toward his greater goal.

Still, we have to help students become mindful of their motivations and examine the "why" behind their endeavors. Is the ultimate motivation to "look smart," or is it to improve, grow, and sharpen skills? The difference is in how the goal is framed. Research has demonstrated that when students seek mastery goals and incremental growth toward an endeavor for the sake of learning, they are more likely to stay motivated toward long-term goals and not lose endurance (Dweck, 2000). Overall, we want students to see that learning/mastery goals will provide a path toward excellence, and setting measurable, incremental goals along the way can be used as a tool to get there.

Students also need opportunities to self-reflect on what inspires and invigorates them (Fogarty et al., 2018). Telling others of aspirations can be highly motivating for some students. This makes the abstract future a bit more concrete and reachable. Participating in competitions and preparing for authentic ways to showcase their work can also fuel and energize progress when hard work becomes tedious. Further, you can ask a student, "What refreshes your energy? What inspires you? What do you do to refuel? What keeps you going when you want to stop?" This awareness can thrust a student to keep moving forward. You can also motivate students by celebrating success and progress and providing concrete pictures of success from real-world role models and your own life. Students need exposure to examples of success again and again: Sharing examples from your own experiences can help them connect to a concrete source of inspiration.

Big Idea

How can I stay motivated to pursue excellence?

Objectives

Students will:

- analyze the "why" behind their pursuits and goals;
- learn to differentiate between mastery goals and performance goals and self-assess their own achievement goals;
- develop a life philosophy to showcase their interests, beliefs, values, and "why"; and
- examine their sources of inspiration and invigoration.

Materials

- Handout 4.1: Performance Versus Learning Goals
- Video: "Simon Sinek–Start With Why–TED Talk Short Edited" (available at https://www.youtube.com/watch?v=IPYeCltXpxw)
- Student access to technology presentation tools if needed (for life philosophy)

Introduction

1. Show the clip of Simon Sinek's "Start With Why" TED Talk.
2. Ask: *How might this idea relate to students your age?* Encourage students to think about the "why" behind their education and ultimately toward a pursuit of excellence. *Why should one pursue excellence? What would be the ultimate goal?* Students may complete the golden circle as described by Sinek, with the "why" in the middle, then the "what" and "how" in the outer circle sections. Guide a discussion to allow students to think about the "so what" behind pursuing excellence in school. Does it go beyond "so that I can get good grades to get into college?" Perhaps it is "so that I can continue to use by abilities for what I enjoy doing" or "so that I can learn to be excellent in my field of study so that I can help change the world to make it a better place." (*Note*. This relates to "grit" in Lesson 6.)

Class Activities

1. Introduce learning versus performance goals: Explain to students that the kind of goals we have about achievement can influence long-term success.
   - Performance goals are focused on overall outcomes and appearing smart (or not appearing stupid).
   - Learning goals are goals focused on learning and improvement. These are also called mastery goals (a person strives to continually grow toward a goal and beyond it).

2. Explain that researchers have found that both kinds of goals lead to positive outcomes, but there are some key differences between them. Refer to Figure 2. Ask: *Why do you think those with performance goals are more likely to worry?* (Those with performance goals are extrinsically motivated by approval, which

leads to worry about disappointing others. Those with mastery/learning goals are intrinsically motivated to get better without threats of outside judgment; what matters is the internal motivation to get better.)

3. There is always something to strive toward in learning/mastery goals. For example, Serena Williams has won numerous tennis championships, but she has not become the "perfect tennis player." With mastery goals, there is always a next level, a step further, something more to learn. (*Note.* The word *mastery* can often be understood as "mastering 100% of content." Here, *mastery* means continuous learning and improvement.)

4. Ask: *Are competitions motivating to you? What are the pros and cons of competition?* Explain that *competition* means "to strive in common." Ask: *How can competition be helpful in pursuing learning/mastery goals?* (Competition can often fuel motivation to reach the next level.)

5. Guide students to link appropriate mastery goals to performance goals. For example, "I want to get an A in French" is a performance goal because it focuses on the outcome of appearing smart. "I want to learn to be fluent in French" is a learning goal because it focuses on the learning and improvement.

6. Ask: *How does understanding learning versus performance goals relate to Simon Sinek's explanation of "why"?* (Learning goals are like the *why*. Learning goals fuel the what, which may include performance goals.)

7. Provide other examples of performance goals, and guide students to understand how to translate them to learning goals. Using a similar framework from Simon Sinek's, the mastery/learning goal is the "why," and the performance goal relates to the "what" (the "how" can be a plan for achieving these goals). Ask students to complete Handout 4.1: Performance Versus Learning Goals. See Figure 3 for examples. In the reflection section, students may consider a more specific "why" than the opening lesson activity. The "why" in this circle should focus on a specific learning goal (I want to learn how to . . .), with the "what" and "how" to include specific ways to learn/master this goal.

8. Guide students to engage in a "sense of purpose" writing activity. Ask students to write about how the world could be a better place. Then, ask students to write about how doing well in school can make the world a better place. Students may share their responses in small groups. When students have a sense for how school relates to their future and world, it can enhance motivation (Paunesku et al., 2015).

9. Lead students to develop a life philosophy. Explain to students that their "why" will continue to develop as they become more self-aware of their abilities, interests, values, and beliefs. To express their current life philosophy and motivations (their "why"), ask students to develop a "My Motivations" or "Life Philosophy" project. This could be in the form of an iMovie, collage, Prezi, or a "featured page" in a "class yearbook," etc., and should include

TRAITS OF INDIVIDUALS WITH PERFORMANCE GOALS	TRAITS OF INDIVIDUALS WITH LEARNING GOALS (OR "MASTERY GOALS")
Focused on appearing smart (or not appearing stupid).	Focused on learning and improvement.
Attribute failure to lack of ability.	Attribute failure to lack of effort (I could have worked harder or have done things differently).
View success as outperforming others.	View success as improving over time.
More likely to have worry and anxiety.	Less likely to have worry and anxiety.
Less likely to persevere through challenges, enjoy what they do, and seek opportunities to grow.	More likely to persevere through challenges, enjoy what they do, and seek opportunities to grow.
Are trying to "prove" their ability (Schraw, 1998).	Seek to "improve" their ability (Schraw, 1998).

FIGURE 2. Performance goals versus learning goals.

PERFORMANCE GOALS	LEARNING GOALS (OR "MASTERY GOALS")
Win first place in the debate competition.	Learn to respond to arguments with valid reasoning and prepared evidence.
Read 40 books by the end of the year.	Learn to analyze the authors' crafts in various genres.
Get an A in math.	Learn to use ratios in real life.

FIGURE 3. Examples of performance goals versus learning goals.

quotes to represent students' motivations for future dreams and symbolic representations of hopes, motivations, and or values (VanTassel-Baska, 2009).

10. Discuss with students the importance of being mindful of what inspires and invigorates them by sharing the following suggestions from Fogarty et al. (2018). Students can make a top five list of what inspires them (role models, peers, coaches, exploring interests, sharing passion with others, etc.) and also develop a list of what invigorates them when they need refueling through

tedious work (e.g., taking a break, taking a walk outside, watching a favorite movie, reading something inspirational, participating in an competition, preparing for an authentic showcase such as a performance, game, art exhibit, etc.). These elements of inspiration and invigoration can be incorporated within the life philosophy project. Students may also include phrases, such as, "I've got this!" "I want to do what she does." "Why not me? If he can do it, I can!" "I want to do this! I can do this! I will do this!" Explain to students that elite performers often have "signature moves" for their work. This might be a certain type of swing for a tennis player, a way a writer always ends a story, a specific way a performer always "pays it forward," etc. Allow students to consider how they might incorporate a signature "move" into their own talent pursuits (academic or otherwise).

Conclusion Connections

Remind students of mindful excellence. Ask: *How does understanding your "why" relate to mindful excellence? How does the "why" help you develop a drive for excellence?*

Curriculum Extensions

Have students examine the motives behind a character (in a short story or novel) or an eminent individual: *What can you infer was the "why" behind his or her pursuits? Was this individual more focused on learning goals or performance goals? Create a 3- to 6-word summary for this individual's life philosophy.*

Personal Reflection

Have students respond to the following: *What are you learning about yourself in terms of your interests and values as they relate to your motivational "why"? How does this self-awareness influence your future?*

LESSON 4: THE WHY FACTOR

Check for Understanding

Have students write a letter to their future selves, persuading themselves to stay motivated toward their goals toward excellence. They should provide solid reasoning and motivation for staying focused on set goals.

Name:_____ Date:_____

HANDOUT 4.1
Performance Versus Learning Goals

Directions: Complete the chart by considering each performance goal. How can you think about the goal differently so that it is a learning/mastery goal? Then, develop two more examples of performance goals and their learning goals on your own.

PERFORMANCE GOALS	LEARNING GOALS (OR "MASTERY GOALS")
Win first place in the debate competition.	
Read 40 books by the end of the year.	
Get an A in math.	

Reflection: How do learning goals relate to your "why"? Choose a personal learning goal and create your own golden circle of what the learning goal might lead you to do (what and how).

Teaching Tenacity, Resilience, and a Drive for Excellence © Prufrock Press Inc.

Tenacity

Setting goals and dreams is one thing; having the endurance to reach them is quite another. Students can become distracted by other interests, experience a setback in their progress toward the greater goal, or even tire of the commitment needed to see further growth. But what is necessary to keep students focused on and determined to reach personal goals? Tenacity—the ability to hold fast to something, to be persistent, not easily dispelled or relinquished.

Children regularly hear encouraging messages about attaining goals: Think positive! If you can dream it you can do it! Never let go of your dreams! Contrary to popular belief, this thinking alone can backfire. Oettingen (2015) studied the negative effects of positive thinking in hundreds of cases with consistent results. Her work showed that dieters gain more weight when they think positively about their future skinny selves, and test-takers perform worse when they envision successful performance. Why is positive thinking about a dream so ineffective? Positive thinking causes individuals to experience relaxed enjoyment while fantasizing about the possible future, developing a state of passivity toward reaching the goal.

So, if thinking positively about reaching a goal is not motivating, then what is? We can teach students to stick to their goals through mental contrasting with implementation intentions (MC-II; Oettingen & Gollwitzer, 2010). This process involves first thinking positively about a wish or goal and the positive feelings and outcomes associated with reaching it. Then, one must think of the obstacles in the way of reaching that goal. In this process, the positive future possibility is contrasted with reality. The mind must figure out how to overcome the obstacles, and the contrast between positive and negative thinking motivates change. The last part involves turning an intention into a plan for implementation. Individuals create an if-then plan to use when the obstacle occurs. The if-then plan allows the brain to go on "autopilot" when the obstacle arises.

WOOP—Wish, Outcome, Obstacle, Plan—is a method that captures MC-II to help individuals examine the feasibility of reaching a goal and the challenges that might have to be overcome (Oettingen, 2015):

- **Wish:** Individuals imagine themselves reaching their goal (e.g., speaking well at a debate competition).
- **Outcome:** Individuals consider the positive outcomes and emotions associated with reaching the goal (e.g., pride, a sense of accomplishment, and confidence). These benefits should be detailed and even visualized if possible, so that individuals can imagine and emotionally feel potential benefits.
- **Obstacles:** Individuals think about what could stand in their way of reaching the goal, especially obstacles within themselves (e.g., fear, being unprepared, forgetting what to say, being too nervous to speak for the group).
- **Plan:** Individuals create plans to meet goals, allowing them to see the specific steps that will allow them to progress toward the goal. The plan is realistic and relevant, as individuals have explored the potential challenges that may come along the way and how to overcome them. It is recommended to say the if-then plan aloud so that when the situation or upcoming obstacle arises, the brain automatically considers behaviors to overcome the obstacle (e.g., "If I am too nervous to speak up, I will remind myself that I have good ideas to share and I will speak my thoughts assertively.").

When students expect success, they are more likely to hold on to the goal and meet it; however, when students do not believe that they can meet a goal, they are less committed to attempting, much less meeting, the goal. If obstacles are too strenuous or out of students' control, students can readjust the goal. Readjustment is better than giving up altogether and can be a positive way to help develop a sense of autonomy.

During this lesson, you may introduce the Reframing Thinking Model (see Appendix). This lesson specifically focuses on the top row. Students consider obstacles that get in the way of their goals (the situation)—and think about what they cannot control and what they can control. The if-then plan applies directly to what they can control.

Big Idea

How can I stick to my goals?

Objectives

Students will:
- examine how factors minimize or maximize persistence toward a task,

- understand that tenacity impacts performance on long-term goals, and
- practice mental contrasting with intentional implementations through the WOOP strategy (Oettingen, 2015) as a means to achieve goals.

Materials

- Sticky notes (several per student)
- (Optional) WOOP worksheets, an app, short video clips, and other guides (available at http://woopmylife.org)
- Videos:
  - □ "How to Make a Paper Transforming Ninja Star–Origami" by ProudPaperOfficial (available at https://www.youtube.com/watch?v=n01fsCDWAUc)
  - □ "How to Make an Easy Origami Pinwheel" by Japanzor (available at https://www.youtube.com/watch?v=muywzgSIaqg)

Introduction

1. Tell students that they are going to do a challenging task. They are going to learn how to make an origami pinwheel. Distribute sticky notes to each student. Decide whether you want students to make a pinwheel and show the related video for instructions.
2. As students work, take note of their response to "challenge." Make some private notes on comments you hear and students' reactions to the challenge (e.g., "This is fun!" "I hate this!" "I'm so not good at making origami!" "I'm completely lost!").
3. After 10–15 minutes, ask students to reflect: *What is your reaction to this challenge? What feelings did you experience? What frustrations did you have? What was your self-talk? What motivated you to keep going? Did you want to give up? Why?*

Class Activities

1. Display the word *tenacity*. Circle "ten," and explain that the root is "tenacitus." English words with "ten" and "tain" relate to its meaning. Ask students to list other words that also have this root (e.g., *attention, tenacious, maintain,*

abstain, tendency, sustain). Ask: *What do you think the Latin word "tenacitus" means?* (It means "holding fast, gripping, clingy, firm, steadfast.")

2. Tenacity means "the quality of holding fast; persistence." Ask students: *What influenced you to keep working on the origami? What would have influenced you to give up? Based on this activity alone, what influences tenacity toward a task?* (Guide students to understand that factors such as motivation, interest, having a set goal, and the belief about your own abilities can influence whether a person persists on a task.)

3. Ask: *Can a person become more tenacious? What would influence a person to be tenacious?*

4. Tell students to envision a dream or any goal they have for themselves in the future—something they believe they can achieve. Ask them to envision the benefits and the positive emotions associated with achieving the goal. Continue to guide students to visualize positive aspects of their dream. You could also ask students to say the goal out loud. Now, provide the surprise: *Psychologists have discovered that positive thinking like this will backfire. The visualization of achieving the goal has tricked the brain into thinking that it experienced the satisfaction of reaching it, which brings a passive, relaxed motivation to actually achieving it. Studies have shown that dieters gain weight and test-takers do worse when they positively visualize their future outcomes and dreams. So, what do we do? Are we doomed? How do you make the dream come true?*

5. Explain: *One way a person can be more tenacious in following through on a goal is to use mental contrasting* (Oettingen & Gollwitzer, 2010). *When people think of goals they want to achieve, they either think positively or negatively about them. The optimists visualize the dream, while the pessimists visualize the obstacles. Some researchers have found that neither way helps a person actually achieve the set goal. It's important to be both an optimist and a pessimist in thinking about your goal: First, think positively about your goal with beliefs that you can achieve it, and then visualize the obstacles so you can clearly create a plan to overcome them. This is called mental contrasting: There is a contrast between the optimism and the pessimism, which catalyzes the action toward the goal.*

6. Guide students through mental contrasting by using WOOP—Wish, Outcome, Obstacle, and Plan (Oettingen, 2015):
   - **Wish:** *Write your wish. This should be a personal goal. Envision what you want to achieve. It should be an achievable wish that you feel you can attain because you have had past success. If you do not think it is possible or you doubt your success, revise it.* (Example: I wish to improve my performance as a runner.)
   - **Outcome:** *Envision the optimal outcome. What are all of the benefits you will experience from getting this wish? Think about how you will feel when your wish or goal is met. So far, you have been thinking like an optimist.*

(Example: I will feel proud of myself. I will feel more energized and feel more confident.)

- **Obstacle:** Remind students that there are many studies that have shown that if you only visualize the positive aspects of your goal, you will be much more likely *not* to make progress. Explain: *Now it's time to think more negatively. Think about the realities of what will hold you back from achieving your wish. What are the factors that will get in the way? What are your internal obstacles that will keep you from achieving your wish, such as getting distracted easily, wanting to do something else instead, etc.?* (Example: I don't have time to run. I'd rather watch TV when I get home instead of run.)

- **Plan:** *Now that you have thought about obstacles, this is likely to create a desire or need to tackle the obstacle. This can be done through an if-then statement. This plan creates an automatic pathway in your brain so that you don't have to fight with yourself about whether or not to stick to your goal. The plan helps your brain understand that you have already decided to do it. Say the statement aloud.* (Example: If I feel the urge to watch TV, then I will not even use the remote to turn it on when I get home. I will immediately change clothes and put on my running shoes.)

7. Have students create a WOOP for themselves. Remind students to reflect on what inspires and invigorates them to keep pushing forward (from Lesson 4). This includes taking a short break, thinking about the success of a role model (e.g., "I want to do what she does."), preparing to authentically showcase work, reminding themselves "I can do this," etc.

Conclusion Connections

Ask: *How do our beliefs about our abilities interfere with achieving our goals and wishes? Think through the WOOP strategy. How do our emotions interfere? How do our emotions help us?* Make sure students understand that visualizing wishes evokes positive emotion, while visualizing the obstacles creates unpleasant emotions or a sense of urgency. This contrast helps motivate us to create a plan toward action.

Curriculum Extension

Have students think from the perspective of any real-life eminent individual or a protagonist in a novel or short story they are reading (e.g., Jonas's perspective from *The Giver*, Brian's perspective from *Hatchet*, Meg's perspective from *A Wrinkle in Time*, etc.). Ask: *What was a main goal for the individual? What obstacles did he or she have to overcome to achieve his or her goals? How might he or she think through WOOP? What might have been his or her wish, desired outcome, obstacle, and plan?*

Personal Reflection

Have students respond to the following: *Reflect on your own interests, talents, and goals. What are your long-term goals? Do you typically think more positively or negatively about achieving your goals? How does it help to think through both perspectives?*

Check for Understanding

Ask students to create a word web for *tenacious*. They should place *tenacious* in the middle and show characteristics, synonyms, and related ideas for the word *tenacity*.

Grit

Grit is comprised of passion and perseverance toward long-term goals (Duckworth, 2016). This takes talent into account when considering outcomes of achievement, but Duckworth also found that talent is only one part of two equations: First, talent × effort = skill. Talent provides the starting point, and effort only makes a person better and stronger within the area of talent, allowing for skill development. Then, skill × effort = achievement. Our efforts allow us to build upon our skills and lead us toward achievement. As Duckworth noted, effort makes skills productive; this is where we see the fruits of the talent and labor. Simone Biles started gymnastics at a young age, but she was not an Olympian until more than a decade later. She spent concerted time in the gym, sacrificing school functions and social activities for more hours of deliberate practice to refine her skills. As Biles's efforts increased, so did her skills. With the increased level of skills paired with sustained effort, her achievements were actualized. Biles has grit. She had a long-term goal and a passion, and she took logical actions contributing to her personal development and achievement.

Although grit can facilitate high performance, keep in mind that students are not going to be gritty about taking standardized state tests. Students are unlikely to display grit as they work on math homework problems. We can teach them to persevere, but to reiterate Duckworth's (2016) definition, grit is passion and perseverance toward a *long-term* goal.

We can't just tell a student to "get more grit" or that a student "just needs more grit" in order to succeed. The perseverance part of grit involves facing obstacles, setbacks, and dealing with failure, so we must support students with the environment and resources to allow grit to develop. We must allow them to "fail forward" and provide the safety net for the risk-taking that learning involves. Facing challenges allows students to build resilience; when faced with challenges, they have opportunities to develop skills to push through the pain or frustration of setbacks. Students learn that they can do it—they can meet the high expectations set for them. The modeled expectations and provided opportunities allow students to experience and build qualities that will support the growth of grit. In addition, we can weave grit into our classroom culture by ensuring that students have the resources that they need to reach goals (Barseghian, 2013). Students may experience frustration that halts goal attainment when they feel that they do not have the necessary resources to progress.

In summary, here is a quick list of tips to promote gritty classrooms:

- Offer challenging curriculum.
- Maintain high expectations.
- Provide opportunities to nurture student interests.
- Provide access to needed resources.
- Provide support when students "fail."

Big Idea

What does it mean to be "gritty"?

Objectives

Students will:

- be able to define *grit* and analyze how grit is developed, and
- understand that grit is important for achieving long-term goals.

Materials

- Video: "Grit: The Power of Passion and Perseverance" by Angela Duckworth (available at https://www.ted.com/talks/angela_lee_duckworth_grit_the_power_of_passion_and_perseverance)
- Student access to "Grit Scale" (available at https://angeladuckworth.com/grit-scale)
- (Optional) Student access to "What Is Grit? 5 Signs You Have It and 4 Tips for Developing It" (available at http://www.personalityperfect.com/grit-5-signs-4-tips-developing)

Introduction

1. Ask students to stand on one leg, holding the other leg behind them with their arms. Consider having a competition to see how long students can stand on one leg. (Other options include practicing juggling with two balls, then three, standing in a yoga tree pose, and/or memorizing 13 random digits in a row.)

2. After students try to do this and fail, ask them to try again, and again, focusing on improvement. Ask: *What causes you to get better?* (Learning from mistakes, adjusting strategy by adjusting balance, etc.)

3. Explain that in this lesson students will explore *grit*. Write the term on the board. Grit is perseverance and passion toward long-term goals (Duckworth, 2016). Say: *Obviously, you may not have a long-term goal to stand on one leg, and you may not have a passion for standing on one leg, but we can learn something about goals and perseverance from this exercise. How does this illustration help us understand persevering toward a goal?* (It involves adjustment of strategies, learning from mistakes, working through failure, maintaining focus, etc.)

Class Activities

1. Hold a mini-debate. Students may stand on opposite sides of the room to discuss ideas: *Which is more important to success—talent or effort?*

2. Afterward, explain that Angela Duckworth (2016) proposed an equation for achievement. Show students the following blank equations. Ask them to fill in what they think the equations might be, using the words *effort*, *talent*, and *skill* (two words will be used more than once).

$$\underline{\hspace{3cm}} \times \underline{\hspace{3cm}} = \underline{\hspace{3cm}}$$
$$\underline{\hspace{3cm}} \times \underline{\hspace{3cm}} = \text{achievement}$$

3. Discuss interpretations of the term *talent*. Show the correct equations: talent × effort = skill; skill × effort = achievement. Explain that according to this idea, effort matters twice. According to Duckworth (2016), "Talent—how fast we improve in skill—absolutely matters. But effort factors into the calculations twice, not once. Effort builds skill. At the very same time, effort makes skill productive" (p. 42).

4. Ask students if they can think of any examples in which these equations might apply. For example, a piano player practices technique and improves skill over time (musical ability × effort = skill). The first time these technical exercises are done, they are difficult, but over time, skill improves. As more effort is applied to improving the skill, the piano player achieves higher levels of performances (effort × skill = achievement).

5. Ask students to write down what they want to be when they grow up *and* why. Then, ask students to evaluate the motives: *Does your response show that you are self-oriented (because I really like fashion, because I have fun doing it, because I'm good at it, because I really enjoy it), or other-oriented (because I want to help others), or both (because I have always loved _____ and I would be helping _____)?* A person is more likely to persevere to achieve a goal if the goal is purposeful. If students did not write down an "other-oriented" motive, encourage them to think about a greater purpose. Explain that according to research, people who show *both* types of motives are more likely to persevere and be motivated for the long-term.

6. Show students Duckworth's famous TED Talk, "Grit: The Power of Passion and Perseverance." You may also ask students to read a selected article about grit (see Materials list).

7. Afterward, ask students to summarize the key points of grit by (1) creating a title for the piece they watched/read, (2) listing the three main points from the piece, (3) recording a meaningful quote from the piece, and (4) identifying a symbol to represent the main idea.

8. Allow students to complete the Grit Scale (see Materials list). After discussing results, emphasize that people can learn to get "grittier." Grit is developed through practice, developing an interest, hope, optimism, and mindset.

9. Revisit the introductory activity (i.e., standing on one leg, memorizing random digits, etc.). Ask: *In what ways is this illustration relevant to what we have learned about grit? In what ways is it not relevant?* (Think metaphorically—what might standing on one leg symbolize? A long-term goal. The intro activity lacks some relevance because it does not involve passion toward a long-term goal.)

10. If students completed an Eminent Investigation (see Lesson 3), allow students to note examples of how their individual displayed attributes of grit.

11. Introduce students to the idea "lean in and push through." Explain: *Self-awareness of unpleasant emotion can help you manage your response to the emotion. Struggle feels uncomfortable. Instead of suppressing unpleasant emotions, it is important to lean into the feeling of struggle and know that it is only a temporary uncomfortable feeling. Be aware of the discomfort of doing something challenging. Then, if there is no major threat, step out of your comfort zone into the*

challenge. Push through the discomfort toward courage. Ask students to develop an illustration for the concept.

Conclusion Connections

Connect back to mindful excellence. Ask: *How do our thoughts influence grit? How do our emotions interfere with us developing grit? How can this awareness help you get grittier?* Remind students that grit can involve dealing with unpleasant emotions related to dealing with a challenge (e.g., frustration, fear, etc.).

Curriculum Extension

Have students think about a character in a short story or novel they have recently read: *In a short written response, explain how this character showed elements of grit. Provide evidence to show how the character pursued a long-term goal with passion and perseverance. Also include how the character maximized his or her talents by applying effort and skill. Use Duckworth's equations in supporting you answer: talent × effort = skill; skill × effort = achievement.* (*Note.* This may alternatively be assigned as small group discussion.)

Personal Reflection

Have students respond to the following: *Think about the equations* talent × effort = skill *and* skill × effort = achievement. *Which area (specific academic, athletic, musical, artistic, or other area) in your life might these apply to? Explain how talent is transformed into achievement using these equations.*

Check for Understanding

Have students develop a motto or bumper sticker to show the idea of "grit."

Face-to-Face With Obstacles

Resilience, grit, and tenacity do not develop from taking an easy path to success. This process involves encountering obstacles along the way. Sometimes, the obstacles have to do with our circumstances that are out of our control, but sometimes the obstacle is something within ourselves that we can tackle, if we have the self-awareness to do so.

According to Oettingen's (2015) WOOP process (see Lesson 5), obstacles are important for students to conceptualize on the way to successfully reaching goals. It can be hard to push through obstacles. In many cases, there may be a smaller, short-term reward that can be attained if an individual decides to avoid facing an obstacle. Walter Mischel (2014) is a psychologist known for his "marshmallow test" that examined how children approach obstacles and delay gratification. His research was simple: A researcher presents a marshmallow or other desired treat to a preschooler. The researcher says that she has to go take care of something and will be back soon. If the child can wait until she returns to eat the treat, then the researcher will give the child another treat, doubling the amount. The child is given the option of ringing a bell to signal the researcher to come back and permit the child to eat the first presented treat. The researcher leaves for less than 15 minutes, but this is perceived as quite a long time for these youngsters. The children have to find ways to occupy time on their own and distract themselves from the enticing treat. Some children play with the treat; some dance around; some close their eyes. Children use a variety of methods to distract themselves to persevere toward the goal—a double treat. But not all children can manage this time; some children tap the bell, signaling for the researcher to return early, and eat the single treat.

The single treat is a visible obstacle in the way of the larger goal—two treats. Mischel's research (see Mischel, Shoda, & Rodriguez, 1989) showed that children who were able to wait longer for the two treats tend to do better academically, are more socially adjusted, and have better overall health. The ability to delay gratification in the early years translates to long-term success later in life. Can we teach students how to delay gratification (e.g., hanging out with friends instead of doing homework) for the more satisfying, fulfilling reward of achievement and learning? Yes! Mischel's experiments and many others provide insight as to how to nurture such self-control:

1. **Teach students to think of the future concretely and think of temptations abstractly.** For example, when the preschoolers were able to delay immediate gratification, they envisioned the marshmallow as a cloud or thought about it with a frame around it. When they thought of it in more concrete terms (tasty, sweet, soft), they could not resist the temptation. We can encourage students to make their abstract futures concrete with strong visualizations of their future selves. They can envision what it feels like to achieve successful outcomes (as in the WO of WOOP). "Temptations," such as other competing priorities or distractions, can be framed as obstacles in the way of a more long-term goal.

2. **Emphasize, model, and reinforce that effort leads to success.** When students expect that their efforts will lead to success, the self-control will be worth it. If efforts never lead to success, students will logically choose a reward that is immediate and gratifying, as it is not worth waiting for a reward that is not guaranteed.

3. **Teach students to create specific if-then plans** for when temptations/obstacles arise (as in the P of WOOP).

4. **Cultivate the belief that we can change and control our behaviors.** This sense of control creates a sense of self-efficacy for managing behaviors and outcomes (see Lesson 10).

5. **Teach impulse-control strategies** (see Lesson 19), such as counting backward from 100 (by 7s), as a method to handle intense emotions that may be obstacles in the pursuit of a long-term goal.

6. **Teach students to see themselves and the temptations/obstacles objectively,** like a fly on the wall. By seeing a situation objectively, one can regulate intense emotions associated with a need for immediate gratification.

During this lesson, revisit the Reframing Thinking Model (see Appendix). This lesson continues to focus on the top row. Students consider obstacles that get in the way of their goals (the situation), thinking about what they cannot control and what they can control. The WOOP strategy and the PACT problem-solving strategy relate directly to what a student can control. Ask students to link these ideas to the generalizations about perseverance (perseverance is rooted in purpose; to persevere is to channel enthusiasm into endurance).

Big Idea

What's holding me back?

Objectives

Students will:
- examine types of obstacles standing in the way of meeting established goals and create plans for overcoming various types of obstacles; and
- learn techniques for self-control and evaluate which ones are personally meaningful.

Materials

- Handout 7.1: Overcoming Obstacles
- (Optional) Handout 15.1: PACT Problem Solving
- Video of Walter Mischel's marshmallow experiment (such as "Kids, Marshmallows and the Psychology of Self Control," available at https://www.cnn.com/videos/tv/2015/07/10/marshmallow-test-one-dnt-ac.cnn)

Introduction

Ask: *If things go just right, what will your life look like in 10 years . . . in one year . . . tomorrow?* Students may share aloud and/or reflect in writing. *What are some things that could prevent you from reaching this vision between today and tomorrow . . . between today and one year . . . between today and 10 years? Of these obstacles, what's within your control, and what's out of your control? Why is it important to know the difference?* Guide students to understand that sometimes obstacles (e.g., a distraction, lack of focus, changing attitudes, feeling tired, dealing with feelings of fear or anxiety, etc.) hold us back. But many obstacles can be controlled.

Class Activities

1. Hold a class discussion about New Year's resolutions. Ask: *Why do you think people lose their enthusiasm for their New Year's resolutions?* Share that an estimated 80% of New Year resolutions fail by February (Luciani, 2015).

2. Explain that people can be enthusiastic about their goals, yet lack endurance, mainly because of the obstacles they encounter: *Let's imagine that Cameron is preparing to run a 10K. His goal is to be able to run a 10K (6.2 miles) in 40 minutes. He has 3 months to work toward his goal. What are some obstacles that he may have as he tries to accomplish this goal?* Responses may include:
   - Injury.
   - He may not want to run in the mornings.
   - He may not want to run in bad weather.
   - He may not want to run in the evenings when he is tired.
   - He may feel overwhelmed to run a long distance. He can't even run .5 miles right now.
   - He gets a cramp in his side if he runs for more than 3 minutes and wants to stop.
   - He may not be able to stay motivated.
   - He might have extra projects to do and not have the time to train.
   - He may not be motivated to eat well.
   - He might not be able to buy good running shoes.
   - He might develop blisters on his toes and get discouraged, etc.

3. Ask students to sort these obstacles into categories. After eliciting responses, explain the following categories as types of obstacles:
   - **Goal is too big:** The task or goal is long-term and overwhelming.
   - **Inner obstacle:** Something within you keeps you from achieving a goal (e.g., distraction, boredom, lack of motivation, lack of focus, unpleasant emotions, insecurity, lack of self-control, fear, etc.).
   - **External obstacle:** Something related to outside circumstances keeps you from achieving your goal (e.g., don't have time, don't have finances, don't have support, don't have resources, don't have good environment, situation, or circumstance).

4. Explain: *Whenever we set goals, we should have a strong motivation for the goal. First, it is important to think of at least 4–5 reasons why this goal is important to you.* You may also refer students back to the differences between learning goals and performance goals. Ask students to think of a big goal they want to achieve and why they want to achieve it (e.g., completing a major project,

getting into a great college, doing well at a competition—the "why" may be a means to achieve a long-term goal in the future).

5. Explain: *You have to be clear on what you want. Now it's time to make your goal specific. Can you measure your goal? Is it realistic? Ask yourself, how likely are you to achieve your goal? Do you really want to meet this goal? If you don't feel that you will be successful, you may need to revisit the goal or think of what it would take for you to feel more confident about the goal.* Have students develop a specific goal (consider developing a SMART goal—specific, measurable, attainable, realistic, and time-oriented; Doran, 1981). This should be something they believe they can do.

6. Guide students through completing Handout 7.1: Overcoming Obstacles:
   - If the obstacle involves facing a task that is too big and overwhelming, break the task into STEPs (small tasks, time, energize, progress).
   - Make the tasks small, so that once one is achieved, you feel momentum to keep going further. Make the first task small enough that failure is just about impossible. Then add a time element (when this task will be done, or how long you will do it). For example, Cameron could start out running for 2 minutes (traded for 2 minutes of walking) for one week, and then he could run for 5 minutes on and 2 minutes off during the next week, etc.
   - If the obstacle is an inner obstacle, create an if-then plan (Oettingen, 2015).
   - If the obstacle is an outer obstacle, problem solve through the issue. Is there a way to get more time? Is there a way to ask for resources? Is there a way to get support? Is there a way to set up the environment to be less distracting? Can you change your schedule? (See Teacher's Note.)

Teacher's Note. You might additionally introduce the PACT strategy here. Handout 15.1: PACT Problem Solving can be used to think through solving a problem. PACT stands for Problem, Alternatives/Solutions, Consequences, Try One! Explain how PACT works by asking students to think of a problem that is an obstacle (e.g., not enough time to work on a project). Then, model how to think through alternatives for solving the problem (e.g., cut out another activity to make more time, break the task down into chunks to work on small pieces in small amounts of time, etc.). Then, think through the consequence of each alternative (e.g., "If I cut out another activity, then I may be missing out on something I think is important, but it may be worth it so I can get the assignment completely done." "If I work on it in chunks, I may not get to stay completely focused on the assignment and it will take me longer, but I won't be giving up other activities that are important to me."). The last part of PACT is to try one. The plan can be written as an if-then statement (e.g., "If I am running out of time to complete my project, then I will work on parts of it before school, and during the 20 minutes I get home before ball practice."). If the alternative does not work, then explore other alternatives.

- If the situation is absolutely out of your control (e.g., physical illness, moving locations, not winning a competition), ask yourself, "What's my next step?" Perhaps the next step is to readjust the wish or goal. Sometimes, accepting the reality of a situation is essential. Rather than dwelling on the negative of the obstacle, ask yourself, "What's my next step?"
- Ask students to think through the various types of obstacles and plans for their goal.

7. Show a short video showing the effects of Mischel's Marshmallow test (see Materials list). Ask: *What do such marshmallows represent in our lives?* (Avoiding instant gratification of temporary feel-good rewards and holding out for the long-term reward.) *How can you sustain effort even when you are tired and burned out?*

8. Share the following tips with students:
    - **Extend your effort one step further** (work for at least one more minute, write one more sentence, run one more minute, or wait one more minute). This is an exercise of the will. Self-control is like a muscle. Like other concepts in this unit (intelligence, potential, emotional intelligence, grit), self-control can grow; it's not just something some people have and others don't. Your self-control can get stronger, but it takes some practice.
    - **Know that when you feel the resistance, you are getting stronger.** It is often said that the hardest part of running is the first 5–10 minutes: It's easy to give up; there's often a "wall" of resistance that you have to just push through. In academics, when you face a challenge, it can be easy to give up right away when you feel uncomfortable with the challenge. Pay attention to how you feel. Do you feel out of your comfort zone? Remember that this is normal and means that you are growing. Do you feel that work is challenging? You are learning something from it. Do you feel discouraged from the setback? Don't be afraid of the unpleasant feeling. It's okay to feel this way; it is only a temporary feeling. These feelings of discomfort are a normal part of facing an obstacle and overcoming it.
    - **Think through how distractions are obstacles.** How can you set up a situation so that you do not have to "think" about using self-control?

What can you eliminate from your environment to get rid of distraction? How can you trick your brain into automatic success?

- **Eat well. Sleep. Have energy.** When you do not have the proper energy, it is much more difficult to have self-control. Our brains are most concerned with immediate gratification when we lack energy.

- **Think as an optimist and pessimist—in that order!** Think positively about your goal (i.e., the reasons why you want to achieve it, the positive aspects of achieving your goal), but also think of the obstacles standing in the way and what you will do when those obstacles get in your way (see Lesson 5).

- **Learn to see yourself handling temptations and distractions as a fly on the wall.** Learn to see yourself objectively—to see more clearly the situation (without the intense desire to give into distraction). What advice would you give yourself?

Which ones of these are you most likely to use? In which circumstances? Which one can you try today?

9. (Optional) Ask students to work in groups to create a visual metaphor for what they learned about achieving goals in this lesson (e.g., a car on a journey with roadblocks, a rollercoaster with ups and downs, making progress up a mountain, etc.). Students can indicate different types of obstacles (too big, out of control, within control) and how they can be approached.

10. Read the following quote from *Inner Game of Tennis* by Timothy Gallwey (1997):

When it comes to overcoming obstacles, there are three kinds of people. The first kind sees most obstacles as insurmountable and walks away. The second kind sees an obstacle and says, "I can overcome it," and starts to dig under, climb over, or blast through it. The third type of person, before deciding to overcome the obstacle, tries to find a viewpoint where what is on the other side of the obstacle can be seen. Then, only if the reward is worth the effort, does he attempt to overcome the obstacle. (p. 123)

11. Ask: *How does this quote relate to what you have been learning about grit, tenacity, and perseverance?* Guide students to understand the importance of thinking positively about their wish. The motivation to achieve provides a desire that, when contrasted with the obstacles, creates a sense of urgency to achieve

the goal. If you only think about overcoming the obstacle without it being tied to the wish, the motivation wanes.

Conclusion Connections

Ask: *What is the role of emotion as it relates to self-control? How does the idea of "lean in and push through" apply? How does the idea "Perseverance is rooted in purpose" relate to this lesson?*

Curriculum Extension

Have students consider the types of obstacles a character faces (in a novel or short story) by writing a brief response: *What internal obstacles does the character experience? What advice would you provide this character? Refer to the strategies in the lesson.*

Personal Reflection

Have students respond to the following: *What distracts you from achieving your goals? Consider friends, computer, social media, instant gratification, competing priorities, etc. What plan can you make for getting over this obstacle?*

Check for Understanding

Have students complete an exit ticket: *What advice would you give someone who feels like he or she cannot stick to achieving a goal?*

Name:_____ Date: _____

HANDOUT 7.1
Overcoming Obstacles

Directions: Complete the chart to create a personal plan for a potential obstacle. Think about which type of obstacle(s) you might experience and create a plan. Use the top portion of this handout as a guide.

TYPES OF OBSTACLES	WHAT IT LOOKS LIKE	PLAN OF ACTION
Goal Is Too Big	Start strong, but fizzle in motivation; overwhelming long-term distant goal	Create small steps (small tasks, time-oriented, energize progress).
Inner Obstacle	Boredom, lack of motivation, distraction, unpleasant emotion, fear, worry, discomfort, out of comfort zone, etc.	Create a plan: If (situation), then (behavior) situation. Lean in and push through.
Outer Obstacle	Lack of resources, lack of time, lack of finances, etc.	Focus on what you can control: ■ **P**roblem ■ **A**lternatives ■ **C**onsequences ■ **T**ry one! Seek support. Ask, "What's my next step?"

PERSONAL PLAN FOR MY POTENTIAL OBSTACLES		
My Goal:		

TYPES OF OBSTACLES	WHAT IT LOOKS LIKE	PLAN OF ACTION
Goal Is Too Big		
Inner Obstacle		
Outer Obstacle		

Teaching Tenacity, Resilience, and a Drive for Excellence © Prufrock Press Inc.

Deliberate Practice

What makes an expert an expert? Anders Ericsson studied experts ranging from professional dancers to scientists, and he found that experts spend an exceptional amount of time in their craft (see Ericsson & Pool, 2016). Ericsson introduced the 10,000-hour rule: Expertise in a particular area is developed after thousands of hours of high-quality "deliberate practice." This rule-of-thumb of 10,000 has been popularized through books and blogs, but Ericsson has argued that it has been misunderstood. Anyone can spend 10,000 hours practicing, but it will not lead to achievement if a person is practicing what he already knows. In fact, he might be practicing a skill that makes him worse (becoming a worse driver over time with 10,000 hours of bad habits). Just because a student works on math problems for hours does not guarantee the improvement of math skills; if students' time is dedicated to doing problems that are relatively easy without new challenging concepts, this practice will not improve their skill. It's not a productive use of time; it may even be considered a waste of time.

Deliberate practice is a kind of practice that is intentional and facilitates progress toward the long-term goal (Ericsson & Pool, 2016). This involves having a target in mind and a plan to gradually get there by refining the small, tedious skills that allow one to progress to the next step. For students in your classroom, this can mean guiding them to focus on practicing and refining "one small thing" that can help them move the next step forward. Ericsson and Pool explained that deliberate practice can be used by anyone who wants to improve at anything, even if just a little.

True deliberate practice is not necessarily "fun." Deliberate practice involves intentional reaching just beyond the current level of competency. The goal is a moving target, where a person is always working just outside and above his level of comfort and proficiency, the hallmark of working toward "mastery/learning" goals (see Lesson 4).

Feedback is essential to the small steps in incremental growth. Students need to evaluate what they are doing well and what is not going well—and what should comprise the next goal. Our role is to set the stage for students and to be the source of critical feedback when it is needed. One suggestion for effective feedback is to comment on the strength, "One thing I thought was really effective was . . .," followed by asking "What if you tried . . . ?" (Fogarty et al., 2018). This approach acknowledges the progress but also nudges it forward.

During this lesson, revisit the Reframing Thinking Model (see Appendix). This lesson continues to focus on the top row. Students consider how they can be in charge of controlling their practice efforts toward improving over time with strategic, deliberate practice. Also, ask students to link the idea of deliberate practice to the essential question: What does it take to persevere?

Big Idea

Does practice make perfect?

Objective

Students will define and analyze the importance of deliberate practice in talent development.

Materials

- Handout 8.1: What Is Deliberate Practice?
- Video: "How to Practice Effectively for Just About Anything" by Annie Bosler and Don Greene (available at https://www.youtube.com/watch?v=f 2O6mQkFiiw)
- (Optional) Student access to "A Top Psychologist Says There's Only One Way to Become the Best in Your Field—But Not Everyone Agrees" by Shana Lebowitz (available at http://www.businessinsider.com/anders-ericsson-how-to-become-an-expert-at-anything-2016-6)

Introduction

Ask students: *How long does it take to become "great" at something? The 10,000-hour rule suggests it takes a person 10,000 hours to become an expert. How many days is this?*

(Guide students to figure this out: 416.66 days.) *How many weeks?* (59.5 weeks.) *How many years?* (1.14 years.) *Obviously, a person would have to have time to eat, sleep, and have a life. How might the 10,000 hours be achieved in 10 years? How many hours of day should be dedicated to "practice" over a period of 10 years?* (Allow students to figure this out: 2.7 hours per day, which includes weekends. *Note.* There is a widely held misconception about this rule, addressed in class activities.)

Class Activities

1. Ask students: *Do you think drivers with 15,000 hours of experience are better than drivers with 5,000 hours of experience? Why or why not?* Explain that the 10,000-hour rule is often misunderstood. It is not the amount of time a person spends practicing that matters; rather it is the quality of practice. If a driver has a bad habit of slamming on the brakes too soon, he or she may have just reinforced that habit over years and become an even worse driver. Practice does not necessarily make perfect (Ericsson & Pool, 2016). The practice must be "deliberate practice." For some performers to reach top levels, it takes less time, and for others it can take even longer than 10,000 hours.

2. Ask students to think about something they can do really well that they were *taught* to do (e.g., bake a cake, play tennis, play an instrument, ride a bike). Ask students to think about how they learned the skill: *What were the steps you had to go through as a learner?* Then ask students to share with 2–3 other students and look for patterns. Ask: *How do we learn a skill well?* It is likely that students will reveal this pattern—they were interested in learning it or they had to learn it (motivation), someone showed them how to do it (direct instruction), they had to practice doing it—not just read about it but actually do it (practice), someone told them what they were doing wrong and what they were doing right (feedback), someone gave tips on how to improve (feedback), they made mistakes and learned from mistakes (learn from mistakes), and they felt safe practicing. They were not afraid to make mistakes and did not feel threatened (environment).

3. Explain that even top performers and highly accomplished people have things to learn. They have to continue to improve and strengthen their skills. Distribute Handout 8.1: What Is Deliberate Practice? for students to complete.

4. Show the video "How to Practice Effectively for Just About Anything" by Annie Bosler and Don Greene. As students watch, ask them to make note of 3–5 tips for good practice.

Curriculum Connections

Ask: *How does emotion relate to deliberate practice? Would you say deliberate practice involves positive emotions or more unpleasant ones? How might unpleasant emotions interfere with deliberate practice?* Remind students of "lean in and push through." Encourage students to self-reflect on how they use this strategy throughout the week.

Curriculum Extension

Ask students to read "A Top Psychologist Says There's Only One Way to Become the Best in Your Field—But Not Everyone Agrees" by Shana Lebowitz. Have students analyze the arguments for and against deliberate practice: *What are the assumptions of each side? What are your conclusions about the importance of deliberate practice? If deliberate practice is "necessary but not sufficient" for expert performance, what do you think the other factors might be?*

Personal Reflection

Have students respond to the following: *Think about two areas of your life—one academic and one extracurricular. List some of the skills these areas require. Although you may not be ready to commit to "deliberate" practice regularly, you may still consider purposeful practice (practice dependent on feedback for improvement). Create a plan for improving one of the skills you have listed. Use principles from this lesson. Consider focusing on "one small thing" for your focus to fix and seek feedback.*

Check for Understanding

Have students complete an exit ticket: *How is deliberate practice different from regular practice? Develop a symbol to demonstrate the idea of deliberate practice.*

HANDOUT 8.1
What Is Deliberate Practice?

Directions: Read the passage, and then answer the questions that follow. Use a separate sheet of paper if necessary.

Deliberate practice is necessary for individuals to achieve at high levels. It requires a person to engage in highly demanding mental work with focus and concentration. If a person continues to practice something he already does well, this isn't really good practice; it's just repetition. For example, if you spend time practicing piano but only play the parts you know well over and over, you don't really get better at the parts that are harder.

In *Peak: The Secrets from the New Science of Expertise*, Anders Ericcson and Robert Pool (2016) described 3 F's—Focus, Feedback, and Fix-it. These strategies help a person intentionally practice to develop skills further. First, you have to be able to focus and be free of distraction. You have to have a clear, focused goal on what to improve upon. The practice of the difficult skills should be repeated over and over again until the skill becomes automatic. Next, you have to get feedback on what is working and what is not working. Those who improve work on their weaknesses, not just what they are good at. You have to seek out feedback to understand what these areas of weaknesses are and where you need help. After receiving the feedback, you have to focus on fixing the issues. Again, instead of practicing what you already do well, this involves using mental energy to strategically improve your areas of weakness. Deliberate practice is usually mentally exhausting work; this is why so few people actually do it. It requires such mental energy that a person can only handle so much before taking a break.

1. Have you ever learned to do something, but learned to do it wrong (e.g., play a piano piece, typing skills, throwing a ball)? What is the effect of learning it the wrong way? Why do you think it is so difficult to unlearn this? How could you apply deliberate practice to improve?

HANDOUT 8.1: What Is Deliberate Practice?, *continued*

2. Take about 8–10 minutes to try to memorize a challenging list (first 20 digits of pi, list of presidents, etc.). Apply principles of deliberate practice, including the 3 F's (work with a partner if needed). What was difficult about deliberate practice? What strategies did you use? What strategies will you readjust to continue working on your goal?

3. How can you apply deliberate practice to a personal goal?

Getting in the Flow

When students experience the optimal balance of challenge paired with skill, the stage is set for great things to happen in the classroom. Students can move past mere engagement with a task and enter a state of flow (Csikszentmihalyi, 2008). In flow, individuals are completely absorbed by a task, experiencing challenge that feels effortless. A student writer enters a state of flow as the ideas for a creative writing piece pour from the mind to the page. The intensity of focus and direction is paramount; she knows her goal and has determined the path to it. Everything seems to come together automatically—and happiness is a byproduct of the intentional focus and progress that occur in the flow state.

What can you do to facilitate flow in your classroom? Provide contexts that are appropriately challenging and fit the unique skill sets of your students. You can be aware of and intentionally differentiate according to student readiness levels and help students to become self-aware of when they experience flow. Flow happens at just the right amount of challenge, a place just beyond their comfort level.

To help students self-monitor and reflect on flow states, allow students to verbalize and visualize their thinking during the flow experience. Ask them about the strategies used and the thoughts behind their choices and actions. Help students determine what choices moved them forward and what conditions set the stage for their feeling of "in the moment." Microstates of flow (getting lost in the moment) can happen while reading a book, while doing homework problems, while engaging in thoughtful discussion, or while working on a project for school. Help students become self-aware of when these moments happen. This is right in line with mindful excellence: When they are aware of the emotions associated with flow, students can find opportunities that result in experiences that are appropriately challenging.

To link flow to other concepts presented in Part I, ask students how flow supports the idea that "To persevere is to channel enthusiasm into endurance." Guide students to understand that the state of "flow" allows for a pleasant automatized experience of perseverance—the goal or purposeful task is in the perfect Goldilocks place of challenge. This allows for perseverance to be an enjoyable, even exhilarating, experience.

Big Idea

What is the relationship between work and happiness?

Objective

Students will analyze the circumstances that create flow experiences in a variety of domains.

Materials

- Handout 9.1: Getting in the Flow Zone
- "Challenge vs. Skill" graphic (or "Mental states in Csikszentmihalyi's flow model"; available at https://en.wikipedia.org/wiki/File:Challenge_vs_skill. svg; to display)
- Various levels of Sudoku puzzles available for student choice (accessible online or various Sudoku books)

Introduction

1. Ask: *What if we took a survey and asked 100 people, what is the secret to happiness? What kinds of responses might we get? Let's do a mini-survey in class. Ask at least 10 peers what they think the secret to happiness is.*
2. Share this quote from Benjamin Disraeli: "Action may not always bring happiness, but there is no happiness without action." Ask: *Do you agree or disagree, and why?*
3. Explain that a famous psychologist, Mihaly Csikszentmihalyi (Mee-hi Cheeksent-me-hi), studies happiness and creativity. He believes people are exceptionally happy when they are in a state of flow.

Class Activities

1. Show students the mental states in Csikszentmihalyi's flow model (see Materials list). (*Note.* The image can also be found on Wikipedia under "Mihaly Csikszentmihalyi.")

2. Ask: *If you have a low skill level and are presented with something really easy, how might you be feeling (i.e., apathy; you don't care anything about it, probably don't want to do it)? What if you have a high skill level in a certain area, but the task is not very challenging, such as coloring a picture, playing an easy game, or reading an easy book?* (This is relaxation, which is a positive state, but it is not challenging or necessarily exciting.)

3. Explain that *flow* is when a person is completely engrossed in what he or she is doing. Ask students to read Handout 9.1: Getting in the Flow Zone. Discuss:
   - How can flow help us think differently about challenges?
   - If you are "bored," what might you do to move toward flow? (Seek a challenge.)
   - Is it possible to experience flow without challenge? If you find yourself experiencing a challenge but have some worry about the challenge, what might your next step be (e.g., practice to further develop skills)?
   - How is flow different from deliberate practice (Lesson 8)? (Deliberate practice is not necessarily a fun, exhilarating experience. It is difficult work, but when a skill is developed from deliberate practice, a person can get into flow easier. If you are learning how to play a guitar, it is not fun at first because you have to practice, but once the skill is developed, you can get into flow with playing difficult pieces.)
   - Would watching TV increase or decrease flow? Would playing a video game allow for flow? (*Note.* Video games would potentially cause a state of flow, but TV would not unless the person was interacting with the TV.) Make a list of activities or circumstances that would increase or decrease the possibility for flow.
   - Can we create flow at school? How (e.g., games at school slightly above challenge level, etc.)?
   - Can you be in flow while reading? (Yes, it may be considered a state of micro-flow.)

4. To demonstrate the concept, provide options for varied levels of puzzles, such as Sudoku puzzles (easy, middle, and hard). Explain that a key to flow is matching skill with a level of challenge that is a notch or two above your ability level. If some students have a lot of experience with Sudoku puzzles, they are more likely to enjoy a difficult puzzle. If the task is too easy, they are

more likely to feel bored or simply relaxed. Allow students to experiment with varied levels of Sudoku puzzles and discuss connections to developing a flow experience.

5. Ask: *Now that we have learned about flow, how does this relate to happiness?* Ask students to explain the extent to which Csikszentmihalyi would agree or disagree with Benjamin Disraeli's quote, "Action may not always bring happiness, but there is no happiness without action."

6. Encourage students to be aware of when they are in a "flow" state over the next 3 days. Ask students to jot down these moments in a journal and reflect on the types of experiences and emotions related to the flow state.

Conclusion Connections

Ask: *How does the concept of "lean in and push through" relate to flow?* (The feeling of doing tasks 1–2 notches above your ability level can feel a bit uncomfortable, but after leaning into this struggle, you can step out of your comfort zone and rise up to try to meet that challenge; this results in flow.) *How do thoughts interfere with obtaining flow?* (Sometimes self-doubt, self-criticism, or the belief that "I can't do this" can keep us from getting to flow.)

Curriculum Extension

Have students read about and research Abraham Maslow's concept of "peak" experiences: *Compare Csikszentmihalyi's flow theory to Maslow's idea of "peak." How are they alike? How are they different?*

Personal Reflection

Have students respond to the following: *What new insight do you have about "challenge"? How do emotions relate to flow? In what ways might you enhance the possibilities for "flow"?*

Check for Understanding

Ask students to develop a mindmap to show the meaning of *flow*. They should write the word in the center of their paper (with medium/large handwriting) and draw extensions of ideas that relate to flow. (See http://www.mindmapping.com for examples.)

HANDOUT 9.1
Getting in the Flow Zone

Directions: Read the passage, and then answer the questions that follow. Use a separate sheet of paper if necessary.

Have you ever been so focused on a task that time goes by in what feels like a second? You may be experiencing *flow*, which occurs when individuals are so extremely concentrated on a task that they "get in a zone," where they know exactly what they need to do next. Every second of flow feels effortless because a person is so involved in the activity and knows step by step what to do. This might happen when a person is playing a musical instrument, playing a sport, running, writing, or doing any kind of work. In flow, there is automatic thinking, a sense of joy, and a feeling that you can keep going and do more. When individuals are in flow, they feel a sense of happiness because they are getting immediate feedback from listening to the right musical notes they are playing, writing the best words on a page, or getting in sync in a sport or game. This sense of doing the task well is motivation to keep moving forward. This can produce a sense of elation and thrill. It can also create a sense of clarity and calmness.

These pleasant emotions happen in flow because a person is so focused on the task that there is little distraction, so all energy is focused on what needs to be done. Skills are just right for the task. Because all thoughts are aimed towards the task, thoughts are not aimed towards the self—a person is not worried about his or her own needs or thoughts. This is what creates a sense of timelessness, where the focus on the present is so intense that time seems to fly by.

Flow only happens when there is a right amount of challenge matched with the right amount of skill. If a person has a high level of skill, he or she is not going to experience flow with an easy task. Instead, he would experience boredom. If a person has a low skill level but does something really challenging, the person will likely get frustrated or anxious. Flow happens when a person is doing something just outside his or her comfort zone. It's a place where there is a stretch just a notch above your comfort level. The experience of flow is a reward in and of itself, so people who experience flow want to experience it over and over again.

Note. Adapted from Csikszentmihalyi, 2008

1. Explain the relationship between flow and emotion.

Name: _____ Date: _____

HANDOUT 9.1: Getting in the Flow Zone, *continued*

2. What activities do you do that involve "flow"? How would you rate your skill and challenge level on those activities? How can you use ideas of "flow" to help you grow?

PART II

Growing Toward Excellence

Essential Question

How can I grow beyond the boundaries of my comfort zone?

Big Ideas

- Growth involves risk and courage.
- Growth can be uncomfortable.

LESSON	KEY QUESTION	CONCEPTS
Lesson 10: Growth Mindset	Is intelligence changeable?	Academic perseverance Self-motivation Growth mindset
Lesson 11: Pursuit of Excellence Versus Perfectionism	Is perfectionism harmful or helpful?	Self-regard Self-awareness
Lesson 12: Changing Thinking	How can I change my thinking to change my feelings?	Self-awareness Reality-testing
Lesson 13: Facing the Fear of Failure	How does risk relate to success?	Academic perseverance Flexibility

LESSON	KEY QUESTION	CONCEPTS
Lesson 14: Handling Mistakes	How can I constructively respond to mistakes?	Academic perseverance Flexibility Independence
Lesson 15: Dealing With Setbacks	How can I deal with setbacks?	Academic perseverance Resiliency Problem solving Flexibility
Lesson 16: Can Stress Lead to Success?	Can stress lead to success?	Resiliency Self-awareness
Lesson 17: From Procrastinating to Producing	Why procrastinate?	Academic perseverance Self-motivation

We want our students to successfully conquer challenging tasks that allow them to progress with their goals. In order to pursue excellence, students must not be afraid to take risks, and they must be equipped to face obstacles so they are not discouraged by defeat. In this section, we address how to help students cope with mistakes and the unpleasant emotions that are often experienced in conjunction with perceived failure. We can guide students to understand that they can push through the unpleasant feelings of failure. Emotions, stress, perfectionism, and even mistakes are obstacles—but they are not blockades. Throughout this section, we encourage you to focus discussion and student learning on the following big ideas: "Growth can be uncomfortable" and "Growth involves risk and courage."

Growth Mindset

Growth mindset is essential for student growth and success. A person with a growth mindset believes that ability can grow, while a person with a fixed mindset believes that ability does not change (Dweck, 2006). Mindset orientations can vary, depending on the domain. For example, a person may believe that his cooking abilities can grow, but not intelligence. Or perhaps a student has a growth mindset about sports, but believes her math ability cannot change. Although we have strengths in various areas, students need to understand that we all can make progress and grow a step further in our areas of strength and weakness. The various beliefs about effort, errors, and ego are described in Figure 4.

Consider the learning outcomes associated with mindset beliefs. In the end, students with fixed mindsets potentially learn less. For them, the ultimate pursuit of excellence is not about learning; it's about showing or maintaining a level of ability. They do not place themselves in challenging courses and do not try new things. They limit their opportunities. Students who have growth mindsets learn more. Because they extend themselves and embrace challenging opportunities, whether through advanced coursework or new experiences, they have opportunities to move forward and strengthen their skills.

Students develop these beliefs as a result of the messages they receive about abilities throughout their childhood. Students are not born with internal beliefs about ability. Consider elementary school: Students are often praised for doing work quickly and perfectly, and are told they are smart by doing so. It is no surprise that "easy" is often equated with "smart." These young learners think that if something is easy for a person, then that person must be smart; but, if someone has to work at something, then that shows that the person does not have a natural, high level of ability. Those with fixed mindsets internalize the belief that if a person has to exert effort, then the person may not be smart.

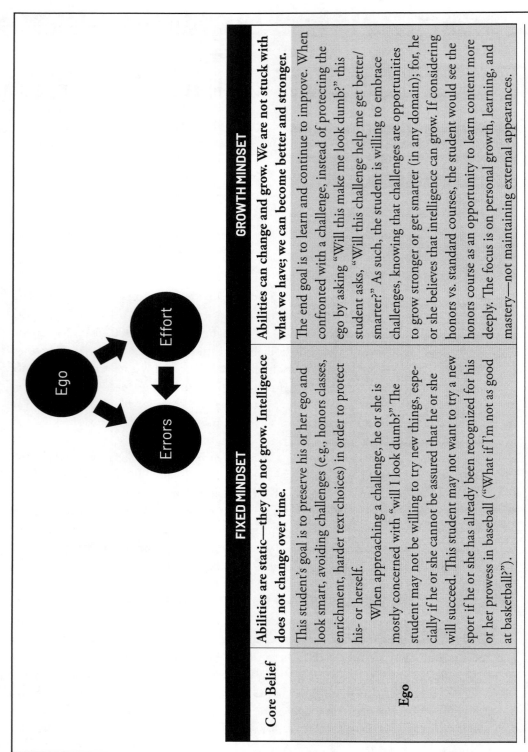

	FIXED MINDSET	GROWTH MINDSET
Core Belief	Abilities are static—they do not grow. Intelligence does not change over time.	Abilities can change and grow. We are not stuck with what we have; we can become better and stronger.
Ego	This student's goal is to preserve his or her ego and look smart, avoiding challenges (e.g., honors classes, enrichment, harder text choices) in order to protect his- or herself. When approaching a challenge, he or she is mostly concerned with "will I look dumb?" The student may not be willing to try new things, especially if he or she cannot be assured that he or she will succeed. This student may not want to try a new sport if he or she has already been recognized for his or her prowess in baseball ("What if I'm not as good at basketball?").	The end goal is to learn and continue to improve. When confronted with a challenge, instead of protecting the ego by asking "Will this make me look dumb?" this student asks, "Will this challenge help me get better/smarter?" As such, the student is willing to embrace challenges, knowing that challenges are opportunities to grow stronger or get smarter (in any domain); for, he or she believes that intelligence can grow. If considering honors vs. standard courses, the student would see the honors course as an opportunity to learn content more deeply. The focus is on personal growth, learning, and mastery—not maintaining external appearances.

FIGURE 4. Student beliefs about ego, effort, and errors.

	FIXED MINDSET	GROWTH MINDSET
Effort	Effort is interpreted as a sign of not being "smart." This student might think that if someone needs to exert effort, then that person must not have ability. Performing well should happen naturally if one has ability. Effort is embarrassing because it shows that someone has to work in order to succeed. If you have to put effort into figuring out a challenging problem, then it is embarrassing because your abilities are not living up to expectations. Effort means you must not be very smart.	Effort supports the development of ability. A violin student with a growth mindset has figured out that her practice sessions contribute to skill improvement. She can play with greater range and fluidity as a result of her concerted efforts. Effort helps you get better. Effort helps you get smarter.
Errors	Similar to effort, errors reveal weaknesses. These students will prefer easy tasks that will not showcase areas of deficiency. A student may choose to take the standard courses vs. honors courses because he believes that he is less likely to make mistakes. When students with fixed mindsets do make mistakes, they tend to blame others for the mistakes and are threatened by criticism. Criticism of their errors chips away their protected ego.	Errors are opportunities for improvement; mistakes actually allow the student to learn more. The student learns what strategy did not work well for the given situation. The student now knows to try something different when approached with a similar problem and has learned from the mistake. Feedback is also welcomed because he or she knows he or she can improve and get smarter. For this student, honors courses provide greater opportunity to extend learning. Honors courses provide greater opportunity for mistakes but also greater opportunity for deeper growth.

FIGURE 4. Continued.

When we support the development of growth mindset through appropriate curriculum, praise, and modeling, we allow students to consider the idea that their abilities are limitless. Their perspectives and actions set the stage for future success. When we praise the process behind their learning, we help students understand that their actions, not necessarily a static ability, led to their success (see Figure 5). This helps them understand the control they have in their lives to make incremental steps toward growth and achievement.

Big Idea

Is intelligence changeable?

Objectives

Students will:
- define *intelligence* and debate whether it is changeable,
- differentiate between fixed mindset and growth mindset beliefs and reason through the implications of these beliefs, and
- relate neuroplasticity to deliberate practice to demonstrate understanding of how "challenge" changes the brain.

Materials

- Handout 10.1: Growth Versus Fixed Mindset Beliefs
- Handout 10.2: Character Analysis of Mindset Beliefs
- 2 feet of plastic wrap per pair of students

Introduction

1. Ask students to brainstorm at least 25 things that grow. Then, ask: *How would you organize your list into categories? What can we say about the concept "growth"? Was intelligence on your list of things that grow? Was creativity? Do these things grow?* (*Note.* Don't tell students the answer yet—but, in short, yes, creativity and intelligence are believed to be malleable.) Students may develop the following generalizations:
   - Change is necessary for growth.
   - Conflict leads to growth.

WHAT YOU MIGHT SAY	WHAT YOU COULD SAY INSTEAD	HOW FEEDBACK CHANGE PROMOTES GROWTH MINDSET
Good effort! Good try!	I can tell that you worked really hard to find connections between the story we read in class and historical examples of X! Look at all of the references you examined!	This shows you value effort. However, never praise effort that wasn't there. This is an especially important caveat for gifted students because many of them do not have to put forth much effort in tasks.
Wow! You're a smart one!	I like the way you thought/created/chose/decided/designed. . . .	This acknowledges the thought processes involved in accomplishing the task. Students understand they had control over the outcome.
Nice work!	Wow! This writing shows that (you really know how to develop characters, you have put thought into shaping the theme, you use lots of descriptive language to develop the setting). Wow! You've got this! You really understand (fractions, ecosystems).	This is specific feedback and acknowledges what the student knows and understands, which emphasizes the importance of *learning* instead of just performance.
That's wrong.	Tell me about how you did this.	This encourages the student to focus on the process through explanation. The student can verbalize the thinking and decisions that were made and see how changes or different strategies can produce a more favorable outcome.

FIGURE 5. Growth mindset responses. Adapted from Parker Peters & Mofield, 2017.

- Growth can be impeded or cultivated by various factors and circumstances.
- Growth can be uncomfortable.

2. Read aloud the following statements (from Dweck, 2006), and ask students to determine if they agree or disagree. They can stand on opposite sides of the room for a quick debate.
   - Your intelligence is something very basic about you that you can't change very much.
   - You can learn new things, but you can't really change how intelligent you are.
   - No matter how much intelligence you have, you can always change it quite a bit.
   - You can always substantially change how intelligent you are.

3. After some discussion, explain to students that in order to really know how they feel about these statements, it's important to define *intelligence*. Ask: *How would you define intelligence?* Explain that, "Intelligence is a very general mental capability that, among other things, involves the ability to reason, plan, solve problems, think abstractly, comprehend complex ideas, learn quickly and learn from experience" (Gottfredson, 1997).

4. Ask: *If intelligence is your ability to solve problems, can this change and improve? If it is the ability to reason, can you improve your reasoning? Can you improve your ability to plan?* (Yes!) *Statements 1 and 2 are fixed mindset beliefs. Statements 3 and 4 are growth mindset beliefs. In these statements, you can also substitute the word "intelligence" for any ability, including creativity, musical ability, athleticism, cooking ability, math ability, etc. Although some individuals have strengths in specific areas, everyone is capable of improvement in any area.*

Class Activities

1. Explain mindset beliefs to students. Distribute Handout 10.1: Growth Versus Fixed Mindset Beliefs (see Table 3), and ask students to develop thinking self-talk statements for each belief in the chart. This chart helps students understand that *beliefs* about our abilities influence our *thinking*. If a student holds the belief that intelligence does not change, this belief coincides with thinking. For example:
   - Growth mindset thought about intelligence: "I can get smarter!"
   - Fixed mindset thought about intelligence: "This is as smart as I'll ever be."

TABLE 3

Teacher's Guide to Handout 10.1

	GROWTH MINDSET	FIXED MINDSET
Belief About Intelligence	Intelligence can grow, change, and develop.	Intelligence cannot change. It is set in stone. It's what you were born with, and that's it.
Thinking About Intelligence	Sample response: "I can get smarter!"	Sample response: "This is as smart as I'll ever be."
Belief About Self	I am mostly concerned about learning and improving.	I have to show everyone how smart I am. I have to prove it.
Thinking About Self	Sample response "I can't wait to learn more!"	Sample response, "I hope I don't look stupid."
Belief About Effort	Effort grows ability. The more you strategically work towards something, the more skilled you will be.	Putting effort into something means that I may not be very good. Effort is not worthwhile, especially if what I'm doing does not come naturally to me.
Thinking About Effort	Sample response: "The harder I work, the more my ability will grow."	Sample response: "If I work hard, it must be because I'm not smart or good at it."
Belief About Challenges	Challenges are opportunities to get better. There is a desire to get out of the comfort zone to improve.	Challenges are threatening and should be avoided. They are a threat to looking smart.
Thinking About Challenges	Sample response: "Bring it! This is going to help me get smarter!"	Sample response: "I hate feeling uncomfortable. Challenges make me feel embarrassed."
Belief About Mistakes	Mistakes help me know what to do better next time.	Mistakes are a reflection of me as a person. They reflect failure.
Thinking About Mistakes	Sample response: "Mistakes are opportunities to learn more about what I don't understand. They show me what paths lead or don't lead me to the desired path."	Sample response: "Mistakes mean that I'm stupid. Mistakes mean I'm not as smart as people think I am."
Results	Sample response: "More likely to grow to potential and achieve."	Sample response: "More likely to stagnate, not grow, be content with the status quo."
Symbol	Student responses may vary.	Student responses may vary.

2. Discuss the implications of each belief/thinking system. For growth mindset, individuals are more likely to reach their heights of potential because they are more likely to enjoy learning and challenges, and therefore learn more. Those with fixed mindset beliefs may be less likely to grow to reach their potential because they avoid challenges necessary for growth to occur.

3. Ask students to explain how the beliefs relate to each other (beliefs about intelligence, effort, self, challenges, and mistakes). You may write these words on the board and draw arrows to show relationships. For example, if you believe your intelligence can grow, this makes you eager to learn from mistakes because you know you can get smarter. Protecting your "self" (ego) by appearing smart relates to avoiding challenges.

4. Explain that a person can have fixed mindset beliefs in one area of life (e.g., art) while having growth mindset beliefs in another area (e.g., math). Ask students to choose an area and develop a skit or comic strip that shows the contrast between fixed and growth mindset beliefs.

5. Explain to students that the brain literally grows when it is challenged—just like a muscle grows when a person works out. Neural connections are made stronger when we challenge ourselves and learn from mistakes and feedback. These connections do not continue to develop if we only engage in easy tasks. Replay the video from Lesson 6, "How to Practice Effectively for Just about Anything" by Annie Bosler and Don Greene, which shows how pathways are formed in the brain with practice.

6. Provide pairs of students with about 2 feet of plastic wrap, and ask them to demonstrate their understanding of strong neural connections. Guide students to understand that when something new is learned, there is a relatively weak connection (with one layer of Saran wrap between two points, when stretched, the plastic wrap breaks), but when a person is challenged and learns from mistakes, their neural connections get stronger (add other layers of Saran wrap and twist). This idea emphasizes that the brain is like a muscle.

7. Emphasize that struggling on an assignment does not mean that a person is not "smart." Smart does not mean the same thing as "doing something easy." No one gets smarter by just doing easy things—and no one gets smarter by quitting. Persevering through something challenging actually makes you "smarter" (or more skilled at the task). This is the core belief of growth mindset!

8. Throughout the year, use pipe cleaners to build a brain in the classroom. Each pipe cleaner represents knowledge related to a unit (e.g., fractions, ecosystems, literary elements, etc.). As students encounter new learning of additional concepts, add a pipe cleaner to connect and visually "build" a brain. Even when topics do not seem to relate (e.g., learning about stars and ecosystems), ask students to think abstractly about the similarities. For example, both stars and

ecosystems are major systems that consist of parts relating to each other (idea adapted with permission from Ashley Kirk, Sumner County teacher).

Conclusion Connections

Ask: *What emotions relate to fixed mindset beliefs (e.g., being comfortable, feeling safe)? How does the belief "intelligence does not change" affect the pursuit of excellence? What emotions are associated with growth mindset beliefs (e.g., feeling discomfort when embracing a challenge, feeling some "pain" in hard work and effort)? How does the belief "intelligence can grow" affect the pursuit of excellence?*

Share the following poem with students and make connections with other concepts (e.g., mindful excellence, tenacity, lean in and push through, etc.). Students may also create a poem about pursuing challenges.

Give me a challenge worthy of my talents
An impossible equation no one else can balance
An issue the likes no one has ever seen
A difficult riddle far beyond the mean
Of what the lazy apathetic and disinterested prefer
I'm in the business where greatness will occur
And that won't happen if my obstacles are lame
Mediocre hurdles? That's not why I came
I came to slay dragons and conquer strongholds
I'm not waiting around to see what unfolds
I'm going for it with everything I can
And if I need to I'll make up a plan
With confidence of action and precise elocution
Providing possibility I've got a solution.

—Jason Tomlinson
(Gifted education teacher, Sumner County Schools)

Curriculum Extension

Ask students to think about a book or short story they have recently read: *In what ways did the main character demonstrate a fixed or growth mindset? Use Handout 10.2: Character Analysis of Mindset Beliefs to guide your thinking.*

Ask students to investigate a more in-depth study of neuroplasticity in the brain. What unanswered questions might they have? What does brain research (neuroscience) say about how the brain grows?

Personal Reflection

Have students respond to the following: *In what areas of your life do you have a fixed mindset? In what areas do you have a growth mindset? Why might this be? How do you think your beliefs were formed? What can you do to move toward a growth mindset?*

Check for Understanding

Have students complete an exit ticket: *At first, I thought . . . Now, I think . . .*

Name:_____ Date: _____

Growth Versus Fixed Mindset Beliefs

Directions: Develop thinking self-talk statements for each belief in the chart.

	GROWTH MINDSET	FIXED MINDSET
Belief About Intelligence	*Intelligence can grow, change, and develop.*	*Intelligence cannot change. It is set in stone. It's what you were born with, and that's it.*
Thinking About Intelligence		
Belief About Self	*I am mostly concerned about learning and improving.*	*I have to show everyone how smart I am. I have to prove it.*
Thinking About Self		
Belief About Effort	*Effort grows ability. The more you strategically work towards something, the more skilled you will be.*	*Putting effort into something means that I may not be very good. Effort is not worthwhile, especially if what I'm doing does not come naturally to me.*
Thinking About Effort		
Belief About Challenges	*Challenges are opportunities to get better. There is a desire to get out of the comfort zone to improve.*	*Challenges are threatening and should be avoided. They are a threat to looking smart.*
Thinking About Challenges		
Belief About Mistakes	*Mistakes help me know what to do better next time.*	*Mistakes are a reflection of me as a person. They reflect failure.*
Thinking About Mistakes		
Results		
Symbol		

Name:_____ Date:_____

Character Analysis of Mindset Beliefs

Directions: Choose one character in the story and complete a mindset profile analysis on the character. If necessary, use a separate sheet of paper to answer the questions.

1. What are the three main challenges the character faces?

2. Where on the continuum would you place the character's thoughts, action, and behavior regarding mindset beliefs (if applicable)?

Ego

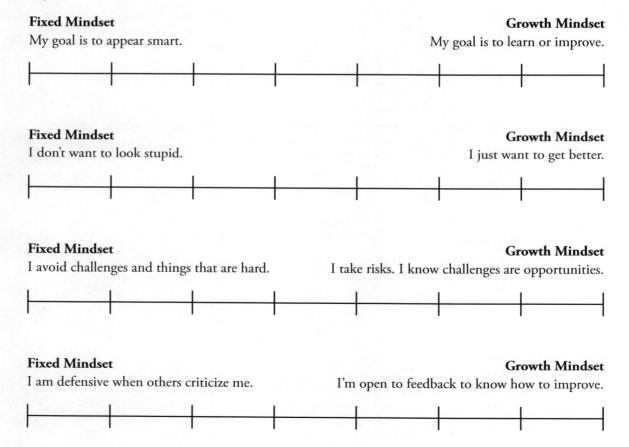

Fixed Mindset
My goal is to appear smart.

Growth Mindset
My goal is to learn or improve.

Fixed Mindset
I don't want to look stupid.

Growth Mindset
I just want to get better.

Fixed Mindset
I avoid challenges and things that are hard.

Growth Mindset
I take risks. I know challenges are opportunities.

Fixed Mindset
I am defensive when others criticize me.

Growth Mindset
I'm open to feedback to know how to improve.

HANDOUT 10.2: Character Analysis of Mindset Beliefs, *continued*

Effort

Fixed Mindset   **Growth Mindset**
Effort is embarrassing.   Effort grows ability.

|———————|———————|———————|———————|———————|———————|———————|

Fixed Mindset   **Growth Mindset**
If I work hard, I must not be smart.   If I work hard, I get better.

|———————|———————|———————|———————|———————|———————|———————|

Errors

Fixed Mindset   **Growth Mindset**
My mistake reflects that I'm a failure.   My mistake shows me how to improve.

|———————|———————|———————|———————|———————|———————|———————|

Fixed Mindset   **Growth Mindset**
I'm devastated by a setback.   The setback motivates me to persevere.

|———————|———————|———————|———————|———————|———————|———————|

Answer the following questions.

1. Provide evidence to support some of your ratings.

Name:_____ Date:_____

HANDOUT 10.2: Character Analysis of Mindset Beliefs, *continued*

2. How does the idea "change is necessary for growth" relate to the text?

3. What does the character learn about life through the conflict he or she encounters? Does this relate to mindset beliefs? How?

4. Think of an example where the character displays perseverance, tenacity, task commitment, or risk-taking. Imagine the character acted the opposite way at this point in the story. How would this have affected the outcome of the story? How would it have affected the theme?

5. Write a first-person point of view account of the internal thoughts of the character experiencing either a "fixed" or "growth" mindset moment in the book. Refer to setbacks, risk-taking, hard work, perseverance, mistakes, learning, or challenges.

Pursuit of Excellence Versus Perfectionism

Some students set goals beyond what is expected or even possible, regarding anything short of perfection as unacceptable. These students measure their self-worth based on reaching unrealistic standards. Perfectionism is historically defined as "dissatisfaction of one's perceived actual performance in comparison of one's ideal performance" (Hamachek, 1978, p. 27). But can positive results stem from perfectionism?

"Healthy," or adaptive, perfectionists enjoy their work and experience joy and satisfaction when striving toward excellence. Healthy perfectionism is sometimes called a pursuit of excellence. Consider many graduate students: They have sought a higher degree to learn about a topic in depth. They likely have high expectations, but enjoy the learning experience. *Personal standards* and *organization* are elements associated with healthy perfectionism (Frost, Marten, Lahart, & Rosenblate, 1990). Those who exhibit high personal standards are motivated by a sense of self-satisfaction. Students high in organization emphasize order and neatness. The goal is to strive for excellence and mastery, and to have a clear plan to achieve this goal.

The difference between healthy and unhealthy/maladaptive perfectionism is the motive. As you work with students, think about why a student is experiencing perfectionism: Is the striving for perfection out of a fear of failure and not measuring up, or is it out of pursuit of a high goal? The following lesson guides students to understand differences between expecting perfection and striving for excellence. Much of this relates to understanding the associated internal thoughts that drive the students' feelings and behaviors. As such, there are several negative thinking styles, as described by Antony and Swinson (2009):

- **All-or-nothing thinking:** *Either I make all A's, or I'm a complete failure.*
- **Should statements:** *I should always be the best.*

- **Magnifying the negative:** One piece of criticism is all-consuming: *I can't stop thinking about her comment!*
- **Assuming negative judgments:** *Because I messed up, people will think I'm stupid.*
- **Need for control:** *I have to double-check everything over and over again and ask for others' approval to make sure it is correct.* Perfectionism provides a sense of controlling one's environment.
- **Catastrophic thinking:** *This one mistake will keep me from getting into college.*

Students who exhibit these thinking patterns may be wrestling with feelings of powerlessness; they have less control than they want and may feel that others judge them. Saarni (1999) noted that this thinking can result in feelings of shame or guilt for not living up to desired expectations. Thus, the thought patterns that fuel both healthy and unhealthy perfectionism are important to recognize. Students' resulting verbalizations and behaviors can provide clues that can help us help them. For many perfectionists, fear is the driving force for decisions and behaviors. We can help perfectionists recognize the role of fear as it relates to perfectionism and provide them with supports to reframe their thinking about mistakes (see Lesson 12).

Here are some tips for helping perfectionistic students (adapted from Mofield & Parker Peters, 2018b):

- **Help students *feel* valued.** Perfectionism can be rooted in maintaining an identity that is reinforced by being valued for high accomplishment and achieving excellence. Do students have opportunities for their identities to be reinforced beyond being smart and accomplished? Give them opportunities to contribute in purposeful ways to the lives of others through meaningful service.

- **Be aware that some perfectionists may appear "just fine" to an outward observer.** They have lofty goals and are equipped with healthy strategies and organization to reach these goals. But they may live with excessive self-criticism and self-doubt, maintaining the belief that self-worth is contingent on reaching excessive levels of performance. Excessively high levels of achievement or expectations of achievement can be indicative of unhealthy perfectionism; educators should be proactive in taking action before maladaptive perfectionistic behaviors manifest into more serious mental or emotional concerns. Talk to students about their goals and achievements.

- **Remember that the primary emotion related to perfectionism is fear.** As children might fear storms, snakes, or public speaking, it is important not to minimize their fear as it relates to perfection. We must validate their feelings and offer needed support. Perfectionists fear failure, a loss of control, a lack of certainty, or the pain of shame. Provide them the reassurance that they need and ask them, "What can I do to support you?"

- **Help perfectionists enjoy the present.** They can be consumed by the past by thinking "I should have . . ." or be excessively worried about the future by anticipating negative outcomes (Greenspon, 2016). Guide them to be mindful of their present emotions and thoughts and to look for moments of joy. A student may have just successfully finished a challenging concerto; support the student to enjoy this moment instead of worrying that he will not be able to handle his next musical piece. Because fear of what will happen in the future can manifest as anxiety, providing a sense of control through a focused awareness of the present can minimize such anxiety.
- **Celebrate success by acknowledging growth and learning.** Although we have cautioned against excessive praise for accomplishment, it is still important to celebrate the means toward accomplishment. In doing so, the focus should be on the incremental achievements along the way and celebration of learning involved.

Big Idea

Is perfectionism harmful or helpful?

Objectives

Students will:
- reflect on motivations for perfectionism, and
- differentiate between unhealthy perfectionism and the pursuit of excellence.

Note. The other lessons in Part II relate to how to deal with the thoughts, motivations, behaviors, and emotions related to perfectionism. This lesson may be most useful with students who have perfectionistic tendencies.

Materials

- Handout 11.1: Types of Perfectionism (one set cut into strips in advance)

Introduction

1. Display the following quote often attributed to Albert Einstein: "A person who never made a mistake never tried anything new." Intentionally misspell a word and see if anyone catches it (e.g., spell *Einstein* as *Einstien*).
2. Ask students: *What comes to mind when you think about this quote? Paraphrase this quote into a short text to a friend, using emoji if you'd like.*

Class Activities

1. Lead a class discussion:
   - Do you consider yourself a perfectionist? What are the qualities of a perfectionist?
   - Do you think people expect you to be perfect? If so, how do they say it? Are messages always explicit, or are they sometimes implied? Why do you suppose someone might expect you to be perfect?
   - What happens when you are less than perfect? How do you feel when you get answers wrong or you receive a lower grade than you expected?
   - What are advantages and disadvantages of perfectionism? (List them on the board.)

2. Explain that there are two types of perfectionism: healthy (also known as a pursuit of excellence) and unhealthy perfectionism. The differences between these two relate to motivation. Unhealthy perfectionists are motivated by a fear of failure, while healthy perfectionists are motivated by desire of success. There can also be mixed motivation (both afraid of failure and motivated for success).
3. Ask students to work in groups of 2–3 to think about the differences between the types of perfectionism. Distribute one strip from Handout 11.1: Types of Perfectionism to each student. Ask students to think about whether the descriptor relates to unhealthy perfectionism or a pursuit of excellence. Ask students to move to the side of the room (unhealthy perfectionism vs. pursuit of excellence) they think matches their descriptor and read their descriptor. If students participated in Lesson 10, also encourage them to make connections between unhealthy perfectionism and fixed mindset beliefs. Review correct responses during whole-group discussion.
4. Discuss negative consequences of unhealthy perfectionism. Read the following scenarios:

- Julie graduated at the top of her class in high school. Now that she is in college, she is competing with lots of other high achievers. Julie can't accept being an average student at college. She decides to drop out.

- Frank never had to try hard in elementary school to make good grades. Things are getting harder in middle school. He knows he can't do as well as he used to, so he decides to just give up. He doesn't feel like he can live up to the high expectations and standards. He thinks, "If I can't be perfect like I used to be, I might as well not try anymore."

- John decides not to sign up for any advanced classes next year. Even though advanced classes would help him in college, he decides to take easier classes because he doesn't want to hurt his GPA.

5. Ask: *What do these individuals have in common?* Guide students to understand that their self-worth seems to be tied to achievement. They have a difficult time with the idea of "failure." They can't bear the thought of failure, so they just give up or decide to avoid an experience altogether.

6. Ask: *Why is it important to take risks in learning? What would have happened if you were afraid of failure as a baby while you were learning to walk? What if you are afraid of failure when you're learning to drive?* (You're never going to drive! Risk-taking is an important part of learning.)

7. Ask: *What is the price of perfectionism? How does perfectionism affect a person's emotions, behaviors, or thoughts? How does it affect a person's body? How does it affect relationships?* Ask students to work in small groups to develop a chart on their own papers like Figure 6. Discuss as a class, using Figure 6 to guide discussion.

8. Ask: *How do expectations relate to perfectionism? How do expectations relate to each type of perfectionism? On a sheet of paper, make two columns. In one column, write a list of expectations you have for yourself. Continue down the column and add expectations you feel from other people* (see Figure 7). *In the other column, list feelings that are associated with these expectations. Do you have any unrealistic expectations for yourself? How can you determine if self-set expectations are realistic or unrealistic? When might it be appropriate to readjust set goals and expectations? How might you readjust your unrealistic expectations?* Give students time to readjust expectations if needed. Think back to WOOP (Lessons 5 and 7). Remind students that wishes or goals are most likely to be achieved when they are challenging but reasonable, and when plans are in place for anticipated obstacles.

EMOTIONS, THOUGHTS, AND BEHAVIORS	BODY	RELATIONSHIPS
• "If I'm not perfect, no one will accept me." • Avoiding challenging classes for fear of making low grades. • Avoiding new experiences for fear of making mistakes. • All-or-nothing thinking: Either I'm going to be the best, or I won't do this at all. • I should . . . (always get straight A's). • I ought . . . (to be as smart as everyone thinks I am). • I must . . . (please everyone around me so that they will like me). • Procrastination: Putting off doing something because it has to be perfect. • Low-self esteem (maybe) if trying to constantly please others.	• Sleep deprivation. • Eating disorders. • Inappropriate nutrition. • Workaholism (someone addicted to work can neglect taking care of himor herself). • Lack of exercise or too much exercise.	• Can be critical of others because they are not perfect. • Workaholism (someone addicted to work can neglect taking care of himor herself). • Overcommitment to activities (band, club activities, church, time to study) causes you to ignore friends/family. • Parent relationships: Can be tense if you feel like you have to meet unrealistic expectations. (*Note.* sometimes these are perceived expectations.)

FIGURE 6. Price of perfectionism. (*Note.* Some information adapted from Adderholdt–Elliott & Goldberg, 1999.)

EXPECTATIONS	FEELINGS
Expectations of myself:	
Expectations from others:	
Revised expectations:	

FIGURE 7. Sample expectations and feelings chart.

Conclusion Connections

How does fear relate to perfectionism? How does the feeling of shame or uncertainty relate to perfectionism? Explain that unhealthy perfectionists may avoid difficult tasks to avoid the unpleasant feelings of uncertainty, shame, or fear. Being aware of how the avoidance of unpleasant emotion relates to perfectionism is a good first step in managing perfectionism. Have students create a visual to show the link between feelings (or the avoidance of feelings) and perfectionism (e.g., perfectionism is a barrier or a shield to protect a person from feeling discomfort, fear, or shame).

Curriculum Extension

Ask students to reflect on the messages of "perfection" portrayed in our society (through TV shows, advertisements, college entrance requirements, etc.): *Is perfection an expectation in society? For whom? Some may argue that there is no such thing as "healthy" perfectionism. Would you agree or disagree?* Have students write about one of these topics, citing evidence to support their claims.

Personal Reflection

Have students respond to the following: *Do you consider yourself a nonperfectionist, a healthy perfectionist, an unhealthy perfectionist, or a combination? What is your motivation behind wanting to exceed standard expectations? How can qualities of "healthy" perfectionism help a person achieve high levels of success?*

Check for Understanding

Have students complete an exit ticket: *How does unhealthy perfectionism interfere with achieving your potential? Make a diagram to accompany your explanation.*

Name:_____ Date: _____

Types of Perfectionism

UNHEALTHY PERFECTIONISM	PURSUIT OF EXCELLENCE
I don't like challenges because I might not be able to be great at them.	I enjoy a challenge.
When I turn in my work, I keep doubting myself and thinking about all of the things that I could have done better.	When I turn in my work, I feel good about what I did. I know I gave my best effort.
I often go overboard in meeting expectations. I might spend 8 hours on a project when most of my friends spend only 2 hours on it.	I try to do my best and strive for excellence. I meet the expectations and do well.
I am afraid of not looking smart.	I am mostly concerned with learning instead of looking smart.
I have a hard time accepting criticism. It makes me feel bad about myself.	I can handle criticism without it hurting my feelings. It helps me know what to do differently.
I am overly concerned with details being just right.	I am mainly concerned with showing what I learn. I try to do my best, even if all of the details are not 100% right.
I feel on top of the world when I accomplish and perform well. I feel extremely upset if I don't do as well as my friends.	I put a lot of effort into my performance and have high standards, but if I don't reach them, I am not upset; I know I can improve my performance next time.
I want to avoid making a mistake at all costs.	I don't like making mistakes, but I realize it's not a reflection of my self-worth. It just means I can get better.
I am very embarrassed when I make mistakes.	I like trying new things. I'm not overly worried about making a mistake, especially when I'm doing something new.
I have a strong desire to be the very best. If I am not the best, I feel bad.	I have a strong desire to excel.
I feel liked, accepted, and worthy when I perform well, but I feel upset or frustrated when I am not achieving.	I am proud of what I accomplish. I put forth my very best effort.

Changing Thinking

Internal dialogue can drive or stifle a pursuit of excellence. Negative self-thoughts can lead to painful feelings of fear or shame. Beck's (1970) and Ellis's (1962) theories of cognitive-behavior therapy can help identify the connections and patterns between thoughts, feelings, and actions. When we are able to understand the thoughts associated with an emotion, we are able to change negative self-talk. The SWAT model may be particularly useful to train our brains to reconsider and "SWAT" negative thoughts. The "shoulds" (e.g., "I should always be the best"), "worries" (e.g., "I worry that I won't do well"), and other types of automatic negative thoughts can be recognized and then changed into "alternative thoughts" (e.g., "I am overall a good student; I just made one mistake.").

Some students' thinking can be consumed with worry. When people worry, they rehearse what might go wrong and how they would deal with it (Goleman, 2005). Worry is constructive when it allows people to plan to solve problems, but, for students experiencing chronic worrying, such as those exhibiting negative thinking styles or maladaptive perfectionism, the negative thoughts cycle out of control. When students make a pattern of worrying, it stifles clear thinking and creativity. Here are a few strategies for supporting students' thought restructuring (adapted from Mofield & Parker Peters, 2018b):

- **Ask students to perform a reality check:** *What would actually happen if you made the second best score in the class? Do terrible things really happen when someone makes an error in a presentation?*
- **Ask students to think from another's perspective (Antony & Swinson, 2009):** *What would your best friend think if you made a mistake? Would he or she judge you and think of you as less smart? Even if he or she did, what would eventually happen?*

- **Help students to step back and look at the bigger picture:** *When I look at all of my grades together, will one B keep me from being considered a good student? Will it affect how I live my life?*
- **Help students find the cause or fear driving their thoughts, emotions, and behaviors (Webb et al., 2005):** *What would happen if this does not go perfectly? Then what? Then what?* The root is likely surmountable.
- **Have students think through the best-case scenario:** *What would be the best possible thing that could happen? What makes you feel this way?* This helps students uncover motives behind their excessive strivings (e.g., approval, acceptance, a sense of accomplishment).
- **Help students understand how worry can be useful:** *What plan can you make because you have this worry? What is in your control? What is out of your control? What next steps can be taken in order to move forward?* Control can alleviate anxiety.
- **Encourage students to tackle challenges and goals beyond self-achievement:** When students feel that they meaningfully contribute to someone else's life, this can bring a sense of value, purpose, and enduring satisfaction.

Changes in thinking take time to establish but can lead students to consider positive alternatives. In this lesson, refer students to the Reframing Thinking Model (see Appendix), particularly focusing on the second row (identify the thought, alternative thought, and next step). You may also direct discussion about helping students understand what is in their control and out of their control (top row) as they consider how worry can be useful for making a constructive plan.

Big Idea

How can I change my thinking to change my feelings?

Objectives

Students will:
- learn how to reshape negative thinking into positive thinking, and
- learn how to reframe thinking about pursuing challenges and encountering setbacks.

Materials

- Handout 12.1: SWAT the Thought

- Flyswatter
- Chart paper and markers (for groups of students) or sticky notes

Introduction

1. Holding a flyswatter, begin explaining that the lesson is going to be about dealing with negative self-talk. Review concepts from previous lessons, and, as you review, start randomly acting as if you are swatting flies in the classroom. *Oh, there's another one, let me swat that thing! . . . Okay, as I was saying . . . wait, there's another . . . let's get rid of that!* Explain: *In this lesson, we will learn to SWAT negative thoughts that we say to ourselves. Sometimes we aren't even aware of these thoughts, but it is important to recognize that they are there because they can influence how we feel.*

2. Ask students: *Is worry ever useful? If so, when?* Lead a discussion on why people worry and some common worries among students in their peer group. Lead a silent chalk walk. Display different categories (e.g., academic, relationships/ friends, family, extracurricular) around the room on chart paper. Students can walk around and silently add common worries of people their age. They may write thought-statements or questions (e.g., "Will my friends accept me?") on sticky notes or by writing on the chart paper. (*Note.* Students do not have to share personal worries.)

Class Activities

1. Explain that we can change how we think in order to change behaviors and how we feel. Students will learn several ways to tackle negative thoughts.

2. Strategy #1: SWAT the "should" thoughts:
   - SWAT stands for "Should"/"Worry" Automatic Thoughts. Explain that it is important to recognize the thoughts that we think. Thoughts influence how we feel, which often influences our behavior. You may use a flyswatter as a visual to "swat" the negative thoughts.
   - Some people who overly worry might have irrational thoughts framed as "I should . . ." or "I must . . ." (e.g., "I should always make A's, or people will think less of me. I must make everyone happy"). Sometimes these thoughts are tied to what people do, so they constantly feel they should be doing something. This influences the emotion of shame or guilt if the

"should" statement doesn't happen. Sometimes after an event is over, they might think, "I should have. . . ."

- Explain that "should" statements can be changed to "I prefer . . . but . . ." or "I hope . . . but. . . ." Write these phrases on the board. These statements are considered rational, while "I should, I must, I ought" are usually more irrational.
- For example, instead of "I must never get a B," this thought can be changed to "I prefer to perform well on my schoolwork, but I'm not an awful person if I don't."
- Students can practice with the following scenarios (or others that relate specifically to your students):
  - ☐ I should be getting all A's.
  - ☐ I must be first chair in the band.
  - ☐ I ought to win a ribbon at the science fair.
  - ☐ I should have said _____ .

3. Strategy #2: SWAT the "worry" thoughts:
- The other part of SWAT is "worry." Like the "should" thoughts, these worry automatic thoughts can be changed to constructive thoughts. There is a reason behind every behavior and emotion. Ask: *What does "worry" help us do?*
- Explain that the purpose of worry is to protect us from danger: *It's a way for our body to signal us to construct a plan. Worry can be redirected to alternative routes to meet a goal. It's helpful to say the worry out loud (e.g., "I'm worried I'm going to get a bad grade in math"), and then develop a reasonable argument for why the worry thought is wrong. Think to yourself, "If a friend were telling me why I shouldn't worry, what would he say?"* You could even ask students to develop "text messages" to themselves from a friend's point of view.
- Explain that worry helps us anticipate problems that might come. Remind students of the WOOP strategy (Oettingen, 2015) in Lesson 5: *If we worry, this means we can constructively make a plan to prepare for setbacks, and the plan will help decrease the worry. First, you can think of what you wish to happen, then imagine the best outcome, and then spend time thinking about the worry. After thinking about what you are worried about, create an if-then statement to constructively approach the issue (e.g., "If I am getting low grades on assignments in math, then I will ask for extra help, practice, and support in math").*

4. Strategy #3: What's the worst thing that would happen if . . . ?
    ■ Tell students: *Another strategy to address worry is to ask, "What's the worst thing that would happen if . . . ?" This often gets to the root of the fear we have.*
    ■ Ask students to think of something in their lives that they are really worried about that relates to academics or talent development (try to get them to think realistically about their own lives). Have students write the following phrase on their paper, "What's the worst thing that could happen if . . . ?" Have students fill in the blank with something they are sincerely worried about (i.e., if I don't do well on my science project, if I get a B in math, if I don't make the basketball team, etc.). Then have students jot down responses to their answers. (Students may share at your discretion.) Explain that in 5 or 10 years, the result will likely not have a lasting impact on their ultimate levels of success.
    ■ After discussing the strategies of recognizing negative thoughts, teach students the link between thoughts, emotions, and behaviors. Discuss with students how our thoughts of a given situation influence how we feel about a situation, which in turn can influence behaviors.

5. Lead students through Handout 12.1: SWAT the Thought, asking them to think about how changing the thought can influence other emotions and outcomes. Note that it is not necessarily "wrong" to have a negative feeling, such as sadness, disappointment, etc. Such feelings are appropriate responses to disappointments and setbacks. However, it is important to recognize that thoughts influence emotions, and emotions can change based on our thinking and interpretation of situations. When an unpleasant emotion is experienced, it is first necessary to be aware of that emotion. Then it is important to reframe or challenge the thought. (Lesson 20 delves further into this.) Use Figure 8 as a guide for discussion.

Conclusion Connections

Remind students of the idea of mindful excellence (being aware of how our thoughts, emotions, and beliefs about abilities affect how we pursue developing our own unknowable potential). Ask: *How do worries influence our emotions? How can reframing our thinking help? How does the lesson relate to the big idea "Growth involves risk and courage"?*

SITUATION	THOUGHT (SWAT!)	EMOTION	CHANGE THE THOUGHT
A challenging assignment is given	I don't want to do this challenging task because I might have to work at it and people will think I'm not very smart.	Fear.	I could try to do this and see what I learn from it.
Not winning in a competition	I'm not as good as people think I am. I'm no good at this.	Disappointment.	I need to keep working harder. What can I learn from this?
Receiving report card grades	I should always make A's. People will think I'm not smart. My life is ruined!	Disappointment, frustration, shame.	I prefer to make A's, but I'm most interested in what I'm learning. Everything is going to be okay in the long run. I wonder what I could do differently to improve?
Not being invited to be a part of a group	Nobody likes me. They're just stuck-up snobs.	Anger, jealousy, sadness.	They may have different interests than I do. I am going to keep being me but still be interested in their ideas. Maybe I can show them I am interested and express something we both have in common. Maybe I should take initiative in making my own group.

FIGURE 8. Teacher's guide to Handout 12.1.

Curriculum Extension

Have students read the story "Eleven" by Sandra Cisneros (or any other short story or novel in which a character experiences disappointment). Ask: *What are the negative thoughts of the protagonist? Even if the self-talk is not evident from the author, what can you infer the main character might be saying to him- or herself? Does the character have SWATs? Provide some advice to the character for changing these thoughts to more positive ones.* At teacher discretion, students may respond in a short written response or in small-group discussion.

Personal Reflection

Have students respond to the following: *In what situations are you likely to deal with negative self-talk and worry? How can understanding the link between thoughts and emotions help you manage disappointing situations?*

Check for Understanding

Have students complete an exit ticket: *How could you change negative thinking to a more constructive thought when dealing with the thought, "I'm not good enough to do this; I need to just give up."*

Name: _____ Date: _____

SWAT the Thought

Directions: Complete the chart by writing a negative thought and emotion for each situation. Then, write an alternative thought.

SITUATION	THOUGHT (SWAT!)	EMOTION	CHANGE THE THOUGHT
A challenging assignment is given	*I don't want to do this challenging task because I might have to work at it and people will think I'm not very smart.*	*Fear*	*I could try to do this and see what I learn from it.*
Not winning in a competition			
Receiving report card grades			
Not being invited to be a part of a group			

Facing the Fear of Failure

In striving toward excellence, students encounter more difficult situations that require courage and resilience to push forward through inevitable failures. Often, it is not ability that thwarts a person from achieving potential, but rather not being able to deal with defeat. Perfectionists cannot move forward because they are too consumed with fear of failure. The unpleasant emotions that accompany failure can keep an individual from leaving a comfort zone and trying something new.

This idea connects to Marsh's (1984) Big Fish in a Little Pond Effect. A young gymnast may consistently win meets when competing against 3A schools. She is the big fish in this case. However, when her coach suggests that she begin competing against 4A schools, she experiences internal turmoil. These are larger schools with a greater number of competent gymnasts. She would no longer be the automatic favorite. She would be a little fish in a big pond. She would have to understand the discomfort of getting out of her comfort zone and deal with these feelings, accept them, and move through them (lean in and push through) in order to try a new experience that would support her continued development.

In order to manage, change, and adapt and solve problems of a personal and interpersonal nature (part of Bar-On's [2006] dimensions of emotional intelligence) risk-taking is necessary, yet we know many students experience worry when trying something that is outside their comfort zone. But, without taking risks, students never get to engage in genuine learning and growth. Students need to tackle small risks, such as trying a new genre of book or sitting with new people on the bus, so that they gain the confidence needed to attempt larger challenges.

Our feedback, whether intended to be constructive or critical, may also contribute to students' decisions to take risks. When students take risks, they are subjecting themselves to a greater chance of receiving critical feedback. They may not be right the first time and will need support or guidance, which may be a new or unwanted concept for some students. However, feedback is such an integral part of learning. Comments and criticism can communicate areas of strength and growth in addition to areas of improvement.

You can encourage small risks in your classroom by providing a safety net for failure, where risks and mistakes are welcomed. Allow students to see that they can conquer small risks, which supports confidence for trying larger challenges. As you lead this lesson, encourage students to reflect on handling emotions associated with risk-taking—to lean in and push through, even when growth is uncomfortable.

Big Idea

How does risk relate to success?

Objectives

Students will:
- analyze the relationship between risk, fear, and success; and
- write a poem about risk as it relates to fear of failure and/or success.

Materials

- A rubber band (to illustrate the idea of "reachfulness")
- Student copies of "George Gray" by Edgar Lee Masters (available online)
- Student access to other related risk-themed poems, such as:
  - □ "Dreams" by Langston Hughes
  - □ "Our Deepest Fear" by Marianne Williamson
  - □ "We Never Know How High We Are" by Emily Dickinson

Introduction

Ask students: *How would you define "risk"?* After discussion, explain that risk is "a situation involving exposure to danger." *Why is risk important to learning? What's "dangerous" about learning?* Guide students to understand that risk is important for learning to occur.

Class Activities

1. Ask students to read "George Gray" by Edgar Lee Masters. Discuss the following questions:
   - What are his regrets?
   - What does "I dreaded the chances" imply in Line 8?
   - What does the ship symbolize?
   - Why has it never set sail?
   - How does this poem relate to fixed mindset beliefs/unhealthy perfectionism?
   - Why do some people fear success?
   - What risks are associated with trying new experiences? Are they worth it?

2. Have students read other poems related to risk: *Compare and contrast these poems, particularly the concepts/ideas, imagery, symbols, and point of view. Develop a chart or Venn diagram to organize your thinking.* You may also ask students to think of popular songs they know that relate to the idea of taking risks and stepping out of your comfort zone, and how this relates to growth.

3. Ask students to think of an accomplished individual (or revisit Eminent Investigations): *What risks did this person have to take on his or her path toward high accomplishment? Would he or she have performed at his or her height of success without taking these risks? Why or why not?*

4. Ask: *What areas of your life—academic, personal (friendships), hobbies, talents, etc.—involve risk-taking? What is the "dangerous" situation in each (e.g., taking a difficult class with the risk of making a lower grade, telling a friend a secret knowing there is danger in that the friend could disclose the secret, competing on a team and letting the team down)? Why is it important to have courage to do something out of your comfort zone?*

5. Explain the concept of Daniel Coyle's (2013) "reachfulness" as a place where we are "pushed to spend time on the edge of our abilities, struggling and reaching just past our current competence" (para. 11). Use a rubber band to illustrate the analogy that one's comfort zone is like a loose rubber band. When stretched to its full capacity, the stretch is somewhat uncomfortable and the rubber band might break, but this is where the real "stretch" happens. We never know what we are capable of doing until we are working at the edge of our competencies. Ask students to think about the risks they take (e.g., running for class president, submitting a story to a writing contest, speaking at the Model UN conference) and how those risks relate to the concept of reachfulness.

6. Show students the following quotes:
   - "Do one thing every day that scares you."—Mary Schmich
   - "You must do the thing you think you cannot do."—Eleanor Roosevelt

   Ask: *What do these quotes mean in terms of growing your personal potential? What does this mean in terms of doing intellectually risky things? What does intellectual risk look like for students your age? What will it look like for you when you are in high school . . . in college . . . in your career field?* (*Note.* Keep the conversation about academic risks instead of risk-taking related to skydiving, riding roller coasters, etc.) Encourage students to pursue learning in their lives that requires them to "try." If students never have the opportunity to sharpen the skill of "trying," they will not know how to get better when they reach the peak of developing their strengths at higher levels.

7. Revisit the big idea "Growth involves risk and courage." Share your own personal experience of taking a risk and growing from the experience. Ask willing students to share times in which they grew by taking risks.

Concluding Connections

Ask: *What emotions are associated with risk-taking? What is the natural response to unpleasant emotion?* Explain to students that an obstacle toward achieving excellence may include dealing with the unpleasant emotions associated with getting out of one's comfort zone. When you feel unpleasant emotion, the first thing to do is be aware of it and explore the purpose of that emotion (e.g., "I'm feeling uneasy about this situation. This feeling is telling me I've never done anything like this before"). Then, as you become aware of what you are feeling, acknowledge the feeling of discomfort and know that it is a temporary feeling of discomfort, but it is also part of what it feels like to be courageous. (More on understanding emotion is explored in Lessons 18–19.) Remind students about the concept "lean in and push through."

Curriculum Extension

Have students write their own poems about risk, regret, reachfulness, fear of failure, and/or fear of success.

Personal Reflection

Have students respond to the following: *What things come easily to you? What are areas in which you have to put more effort? What are the negative consequences of doing things that are only easy? What would you do if you were not afraid (as applied to learning)?*

Check for Understanding

Have students complete an exit ticket: *Why is risk an important part of learning?*

Handling Mistakes

How we cope with setbacks affects the extent to which we achieve (Subotnik et al., 2011). Some students have such difficulty with handling mistakes that they avoid any circumstance that may pose a threat of making a mistake. We can, however, help shift students' thinking about mistakes: Instead of viewing mistakes as negative and evaluative, we can guide students' understanding of mistakes as a part of learning. Mistakes are cues and clues; they tell us to try something different that may work more effectively.

Feedback is, of course, meant to provide direction and support as a student moves toward a target of achievement. We want our students to have the growth mindset interpretation of feedback (see Figure 5, p. 91). This includes a desire for support, direction, and new ideas that come from feedback. In order to foster a yearning for feedback, we must consider what we are modeling for our students. What are we saying to our students? What kind of feedback are we giving to them? Do you praise students when they earn high grades by saying, "Wow! You're a smart one!" or "What a natural!"? Although these phrases come with good intentions, this type of feedback can actually be harmful over time. What will they think when they make mistakes or earn a low grade? Students may internalize that, "If I am smart when I earn a high grade, then I must be dumb now because I earned a lower grade"—even when attempting a much more challenging assignment. Although the person-centered praise may have been intended to boost student confidence, it may inadvertently undermine it, focusing on internal qualities and final product performance (Dweck, 2000).

Finally, understanding how students explain their failures can help us understand how they respond to failure. Does the student perceive that failure is within his or her control? Does the student take responsibility? Or, does the student believe that the failure occurred due to an external factor? When students view both actions and mistakes as malleable, they will also understand that successes and failures are also within

125

their control. They can choose to spend more time studying a topic. They can choose to practice violin with an expert mentor. On the other hand, they can also choose to spend more time on social media when they could be preparing an assignment, but the choice and responsibility is in their hands.

These examples point to Weiner's (1974) theories related to locus of control; does the student feel that he or she can control the outcome, or is it out of his or her hands? It is true that some things are not under our control. For example, students cannot control what the teacher chooses to include on the exam. But students can control how they prepare for the exam: They can ask questions, check their understanding of the material, and dedicate time to reviewing the concepts. They can choose to spend time with the material instead of choosing other activities as the exam approaches. There is actually quite a bit under their control! We need to show students that, yes, they can and do impact personal outcomes, such as exam performance, even when a small part of the situation, the exam content, is not under their control. It is important to help guide students to filter—what is in your control and what is out of your control? Then, what is the next step you can take?

As educators, we can emphasize the importance and empowerment that comes with taking responsibility for actions. We can help students realize how their choices provide them with control and responsibility. These internalized feelings of control can propel students to know the next steps to take when confronting challenges and setbacks. Continue to refer to the Reframing Thinking Model (see Appendix), particularly the top row, in guiding students to consider what they control from a given situation or setback and what their next step might be. (*Note.* We acknowledge that outside circumstances, such as financial resources or lack of opportunity, are out of a student's control. It is important that students feel supported and for educators to advocate for their needs.)

Big Idea

How can I constructively respond to mistakes?

Objective

Students will learn to respond to mistakes, setbacks, and criticism constructively.

Materials

- Handout 14.1: Responding to Criticism

Introduction

1. Ask students to arrange their chairs in a circle. Explain that they will be playing a funny game that will help them laugh at their mistakes.

2. Group students in a circle facing in. In a clockwise direction, students will count up from one. Instead of saying 7 and multiples of 7 and any number with 7 in it (e.g., 17), the student will say "buzz." 1, 2, 3, 4, 5, 6, buzz, 8, 9, 10, 11, 12, 13, buzz, 15, 16, buzz, etc. Once students get the hang of this (reach up to 50), add "zap" for multiples of 5 and numbers with 5 in them. If it is a multiple of 5 and 7 (or includes a 5 and 7 like 57), students will say "buzz-zap." For even more laughs, add "zip" for multiples of 6 and numbers with 6 in them. "Buzz" and/or "zap" can be added (e.g., 30 would be zip-zap).

3. After playing for while, remind students that it's a good idea to laugh at our mistakes. If it felt painful to be the one to mess up the round, remind students that the pain is temporary and it will likely not be remembered a year from now. It's okay to "feel" the sting of the light embarrassment, a typical feeling in the game. They key idea is that they get used to handling the "discomfort" associated with making a mistake. They can learn to "lean in and push through" the pain of messing up the game for the group.

4. Ask students to reflect: *When you made a mistake, how did it affect your approach to the next round? When you saw others make mistakes, how did this help you improve? How did these mistakes help you adjust your strategy while playing the game?* Emphasize the positive of making mistakes: You know how to adjust your strategy for next time.

5. Reflect with students about the experience, noting that this was a simple game to think about working through mistakes. Guide students to list various categories of mistakes people can make (e.g., academic, interpersonal, simple errors, making a wrong decision, athletic mistakes, cooking, etc.). Mistakes are usually a bit embarrassing, but we can reframe how we look at them in order to keep growing and improving. One way is to just laugh at yourself, learn from it, and move on!

Class Activities

1. Explain that in this lesson, students will learn several ways to respond to mistakes or setbacks.

2. Strategy #1: Respond with ownership:

- Ask students: *When you hear someone admit to a mistake, does it make you think more or less of this person? When a leader makes a mistake and he or she admits it, do you think of that leader more in a positive or negative light?* Explain: *One way to deal with a mistake is to "own up" to it.*

- Explain that mistakes can be like a weight we carry that has power over our behaviors and interactions with others. Sometimes it is difficult to admit to making a mistake: Many people choose to blame the mistake on someone else, rationalize why the mistake was made, or feel angry toward themselves for making a mistake. Stephen Covey, author of *7 Habits of Highly Effective People* (2004), recommended that the sooner a person can admit to making a mistake and own up to it, the better. When the mistake can be owned, the person is no longer empowered by the mistake. He or she can move on without the weight. Imagine a person with a heavy backpack (a mistake). When the person can admit to the mistake, it's like letting go of a burden with freedom to move forward. This weight can also represent any guilt or shame associated with the mistake. This can simply mean saying, "My bad. It would have been better to do it differently. Hindsight is 20/20!" or "Oops, sorry about that. This is what I'm learning through this mistake. . . ."

3. Strategy #2: Respond to criticism respectfully:
   - Ask students: *When someone points out a flaw, how do you typically respond? Does it depend on the situation? When you receive constructive criticism on a project, what thoughts go through your head? When you receive constructive criticism from your extracurricular activities (e.g., coaches, ballet teachers, music teachers, etc.), how do you respond? How does it make you feel to receive criticism?*
   - Ask: *What are some feelings that criticism might bring to some people?* Students will likely share that criticism produces negative feelings (e.g., shame, guilt, embarrassment, defensiveness, sadness, disappointment, despair, etc.). Emphasize that this is normal, but we have to learn to recognize that although these feelings are real, emotions can cloud our ability to see value in the criticism. (Consider foggy glasses—it's difficult to see through the fog to see the reality of a situation.)
   - Share tips for receiving criticism:
     - **Feelings versus facts:** Separate your feelings and strive to see any truth in the comment.
     - **Acknowledge that you have heard the criticism:** You might say, "Thank you. I will consider that," or "Thank you. What I hear you saying is . . . (summarize what you heard)."

      ☐ **Reflect:** Look for patterns. Has this type of criticism been given to you before? What are you learning about yourself?

      ☐ **Plan:** Should you change your actions in response to the criticism? If so, make a plan for the change.

   ■ Distribute Handout 14.1: Responding to Criticism. Allow students to practice responding to criticism. They may record their thoughts, discuss in small groups or pairs, or perform a dialogue in front of the class.

4. Strategy #3: Respond with a proactive mindset:

   ■ Explain: *To develop a "drive" for excellence, it's important to feel you are in the "driver's" seat. There are two ways we can respond to the mistakes we make. These beliefs would exist on a continuum instead of one versus another.*

      ☐ **Proactive:** Those with proactive mindsets believe that they have influence (control) over events and circumstances in their lives. This is usually characterized by proactive behaviors, such as putting forth effort. These behaviors relate to an internal locus of control. Those with proactive mindsets think, "There's something I can do about this;" They understand there are some things they cannot control, but focus on what they can.

      ☐ **Reactive:** Those with reactive mindsets believe that they are controlled by events and circumstances in their lives. This is usually characterized by reactive behaviors, such as blaming and wishing. Those with reactive mindsets think, "There's nothing I can do about this, it is someone else's fault." They avoid taking responsibility for mistakes.

   ■ Ask: *How would someone's proactive/reactive mindset influence how he or she receives criticism?* Explain that those with a proactive mindset would see that they have control over what to change in the future. They know they can put forth effort in order to do better next time. Those with a reactive mindset would have a more difficult time with handling the criticism—they would likely blame any mistake on someone else (e.g., the teacher didn't grade fairly, it was an unfair competition, etc.). Those with a reactive mindset would be most upset because they would not feel that they have any control or power to change.

   ■ It is important for students to be able to differentiate when things are really out of their control. If the situation is controllable, then adopting a proactive mindset (internal locus of control) can be constructive. If the situation is not controllable (e.g., disability, lack of resources), then having an internal locus of control interpretation would cause someone to feel overly anxious because he or she really can't control the situation.

5. Ask students to develop skits to demonstrate their understanding of appropriate ways to handle criticism and differences between proactive and reactive mindsets. In their skits, they should also convey one of the big ideas for this section (growth can be uncomfortable; growth involves risk and courage).

Conclusion Connections

Ask: *How does the idea of proactive/reactive mindset relate to mastery versus performance goals (Lesson 4)? How does it relate to the idea of fixed versus growth mindsets (Lesson 10)? How does it relate to healthy perfectionism versus unhealthy perfectionism (Lesson 11)? What patterns do you notice? What feelings are associated with listening to criticism? How do the strategies learned in this lesson help you lean into struggle and push through out of your comfort zone?*

Curriculum Extension

Viktor Frankl, a notable neurologist and psychiatrist, was a Holocaust survivor and wrote the book *Man's Search for Meaning.* Some of his famous quotes include:

> Everything can be taken from a man but one thing: the last of the human freedoms—to choose one's attitude in any given set of circumstances, to choose one's own way.

> When we are no longer able to change a situation, we are challenged to change ourselves.

> Between stimulus and response there is a space. In that space is our power to choose our response. In our response lies our growth and our freedom.

Ask students: *How do these quotes relate to proactive versus reactive mindsets? Research more about Frankl's life, philosophy, and influence on psychology, and share your findings in a creative product. Include other quotes to showcase his beliefs and life philosophy.*

Personal Reflection

Have students respond to the following: *Think about a recent setback you have encountered. How did you handle it? What emotions were involved? Why is it important to be self-aware of our emotions related to setbacks? Would you handle anything differently from the tips learned in this lesson? What lessons have you learned from mistakes? What insight did you gain about yourself from the setback?*

Check for Understanding

Have students complete an exit ticket: *One misunderstanding people may have about handling criticism is _____ . This is what I would say to help them understand it better: _____ .*

HANDOUT 14.1
Responding to Criticism

Directions: Practice responses to the following scenarios.

1. You give a presentation, and the teacher tells you that you need to speak up, make more eye contact, and use better examples in your presentation.

Feelings vs. Fact: What are the feelings? What is the reality?

Acknowledge the criticism:

Reflect: What are you learning about yourself? Is this a pattern?

Plan: Should you change your actions? How might you change?

Name:_____ Date: _____

HANDOUT 14.1: Responding to Criticism, *continued*

2. Your group members tell you, "You're too bossy—you dominate the group!"

Feelings vs. Fact: What are the feelings? What is the reality?
Acknowledge the criticism:
Reflect: What are you learning about yourself? Is this a pattern?
Plan: Should you change your actions? How might you change?

HANDOUT 14.1: Responding to Criticism, *continued*

3. Your teacher tells you, "You need more details on the project. Points were deducted for not following the directions."

Feelings vs. Fact: What are the feelings? What is the reality?
Acknowledge the criticism:
Reflect: What are you learning about yourself? Is this a pattern?
Plan: Should you change your actions? How might you change?

Teaching Tenacity, Resilience, and a Drive for Excellence © Prufrock Press Inc.

Name:_____ Date: _____

HANDOUT 14.1: Responding to Criticism, *continued*

4. Your group members express, "That's such a crazy idea! That would never work! If we did your idea, then we'd have so many problems with our project!"

Feelings vs. Fact: What are the feelings? What is the reality?
Acknowledge the criticism:
Reflect: What are you learning about yourself? Is this a pattern?
Plan: Should you change your actions? How might you change?

Dealing With Setbacks

We need effective coping skills to overcome or bounce back from mistakes. Roth and Cohen (1986) described coping behaviors as either avoidance- or approach-based. *Avoidance* coping behaviors are typically emotion-focused strategies that take attention away from the stressor (e.g., getting angry, yelling, isolating oneself, or ignoring/denying the problem). On the other hand, *approach* coping behaviors focus on the mistake or stressor and take action (e.g., seeking social support, problem solving).

Suppose a student did not do well at a competition. An avoidance coping reaction might include throwing a blaming tantrum (e.g., "It's not my fault that I did not win; it's because the judges have favorites!"). Or perhaps the student engages in internalizing behaviors, such as ruminating over mistakes excessively with "I should have . . ." thinking. On the other hand, a student who uses approach coping would consider methods for future improvement. In both situations, the disappointment is real, but approach coping methods allow the student to move forward. Avoidance coping will not support future success. Approach coping strategies are associated with lower levels of stress, while avoidance coping are associated with higher levels (Compas et al., 2017).

To guide students toward approach coping, have students brainstorm next steps when a mistake is made. Show students that mistakes are opportunities for problem solving. In this lesson, focus students' attention on the last row of the Reframing Thinking Model (see Appendix). Students may consider how to regulate their emotions and reactions to a stressor or setback through an appropriate coping response that will lead to a more regulated emotion.

137

Big Idea

How can I deal with setbacks?

Objectives

Students will:

- be able to differentiate between avoidance and approach coping in response to stress related to a setback or obstacle; and
- apply examples of seeking social support and problem solving to given stressors and setbacks.

Materials

- Handout 15.1: PACT Problem Solving
- Student copies of printable labyrinths (such as https://labyrinthsociety.org/download-a-labyrinth)

Introduction

1. Explain: *Stress is a part of life. We will undoubtedly experience stressful situations. Often, stress is related to some kind of setback or obstacle. This lesson will focus on dealing with stress that relates to setbacks or disappointments (e.g., not doing well on an assignment, not doing well with a competition, being rejected or heavily criticized, something interfering with a long-term goal).*
2. In groups of 2–3, ask students to list at least 20 things people do to deal with stress.
3. Afterward, have students develop categories for their responses. Then, ask: *How do these categories relate to the idea of growing toward excellence?* Guide students to understand that healthy approaches to problems help us move past them so that we can continually grow. Other ways can make the problem even worse.

Class Activities

1. Ask students to look over their lists: *Which ones would you consider to readily address the problem? Which ones would you consider make the problem worse?*

2. Tell students that researchers (i.e., Roth & Cohen, 1986) have explained that there are key ways people "cope" with or manage emotions in response to difficult situations:

   - **Internalizing:** Worrying, crying, holding in feelings (anxiety), engaging in negative self-talk
   - **Externalizing:** Getting angry or aggressive, acting out, unhealthy eating, yelling, blaming
   - **Distancing:** Doing nothing, saying "I don't care," pretending it didn't happen
   - **Problem solving:** Approaching the stress with a plan, figuring out something to do or change
   - **Seeking social support:** Seeking support and assistance from others

3. Ask: *Which behaviors will actually help get beyond the setback?* (Problem solving and seeking social support.) *Which ones might make dealing with the problem potentially worse?* (Internalizing, externalizing, and distancing.) *Why?*

4. Describe a car that comes to the bank of a river and cannot get across it. The driver could *approach* the problem and seek social support (ask for help and advice) or problem solve (consider alternate routes). Or the driver could try to *avoid* the problem altogether by externalizing (sitting there and yelling at the bank of the river), internalizing (crying, worrying, and pouting), or distancing (pretending there's no problem, sitting there and staring at the bank of the river). The driver may need to manage feelings of frustration by taking a few deep breaths (emotional regulation strategy).

5. Ask students to think through handling a problem: *Suppose you are assigned math homework, but when you try to do the problems, they are much more difficult than you thought they would be. This is like coming to the "bank of the river." What would the five ways of coping look like in this situation?*

   - **Internalizing:** Just worry about it all night; lose sleep.
   - **Externalizing:** Blame the teacher; yell at your dog; complain on social media.
   - **Distancing:** Don't do the homework at all.
   - **Problem solving:** Determine what you do and don't understand. Think about different ways to figure it out: look up YouTube videos, read over the book, etc.
   - **Seeking social support:** Reach out to a friend for help.

6. For further practice, have students explore other situations, such ways to cope with getting a disappointing report card, not doing well in a competition, etc.

7. To help students understand the various forms of support available to them, ask them to write the alphabet (A–Z) vertically down a sheet of paper. They should list supports and positive ways for dealing with stressors for each letter (e.g., A is for "Aunt Betty," who is always encouraging, and B is for "bike riding" to handle anxious emotions).

8. Remind students of the WOOP Strategy (see Lesson 5) for when they encounter an obstacle. (Think like an optimist: What is your wish? What it its best outcome? Think like a pessimist: What might happen if something gets in the way? What's the obstacle holding you back? Make a plan.)

9. Tell students that the PACT strategy (refer to Handout 15.1: PACT Problem Solving) is a way to problem solve toward a good plan (also used in Lesson 7). PACT stands for Problem, Alternatives/Solutions, Consequences, Try One!: *For example, when you bring home difficult math problems, you must first understand what the root problem is (e.g., "I don't understand how to do ratios"). Then, alternatives can be explored (e.g., "I could call my friend," "I could look up ideas on YouTube," "I'm not going to do the work," or "I could get on social media and vent."). Then, think about the consequences of the options (i.e., "Which one will most likely help me solve the problem?") Choose it and try it! You can write the plan as an if-then statement. Remember, this is most effective if you think about the positives of your goal first, then think of obstacles, and then develop a plan.*

10. Ask students to apply the PACT strategy to a relevant stressor in their personal lives (see Handout 15.1). Another idea is to ask students to think from the point of view of a character from a cartoon or favorite book and problem solve through an issue the character has.

11. Provide students with strategies to cope with anxiety associated with disappointment, setbacks, or obstacles by teaching relaxation techniques. Allow students to practice these during class time:
    - Close your eyes. Breathe in for 10 seconds, and then breathe out for 10 seconds. Repeat this several times.
    - Tense and relax various muscles in your body. Tense for 10 seconds. Then, release and enjoy the feeling of releasing the tension. (You may guide students with this strategy. Ask students to close their eyes. Ask students to tense their toe muscles for 10 seconds, and then release the tension. Then move to calf muscles, thighs, abs, biceps, hands, neck, face, eyes, etc.)
    - Trace a labyrinth. With a printable labyrinth, use your finger to move toward the center. Labyrinths are designed to help bring focus and clarity to the mind (see Materials list).
    - Listen to relaxing music.

- Practice mindfulness. Mindfulness involves paying careful attention to the present moment without judgment. (*Note.* It is not about calming the mind, or meditating; it is simply about being aware.) You can think about a specific sound you hear, the qualities of a taste, etc. (e.g., eat a raisin and think about every detail, including being aware of your saliva glands, thinking about the process of a grape turning into a raisin, etc.). If judgments arise in the mind or if you start thinking about something else, let the thoughts pass over, and continue to think about the present moment.
- Go for a walk. This releases endorphins, which make you feel happy.
- Take a short break if you are feeling overwhelmed.

12. After practicing one or more strategies, ask: *How did that feel? If you're ever overwhelmed, these are good exercises you can do to feel relaxed. Some of them can also help you fall asleep if you keep worrying about things before sleeping.*

13. Ask: *How does the big idea "growth can be uncomfortable" relate to the different coping responses?* Guide students to understand that several of the avoidance coping styles are ways to avoid being "uncomfortable." The approach strategies (seeking social support and problem solving) are ways to deal with and manage the uncomfortable feeling, but continue to grow. Progress can still be made through difficulty.

Conclusion Connections

Relate the role of emotion to each type of coping strategy: *What emotions are experienced during stress? How does each type of coping response relieve unpleasant emotion? How do approach coping strategies (problem solving, seeking support) relate to "lean in and push through"?* (Approach coping helps you push through and take action through the discomfort. Avoidance coping is a way to avoid the unpleasant emotion. The problem is not handled, and it does not allow you to progress.)

Curriculum Extension

After reading a short story or novel, have students analyze how the character approaches or avoids dealing with stressors in his or her life: *When do you see the character display internalizing behaviors . . . externalizing behaviors? Does he or she approach the problem positively through seeking support, problem solving, or emotional regulation? What advice might you give the character?*

Personal Reflection

Have students respond to the following: *What is your go-to coping strategy when faced with a challenge, obstacle, mistake, or setback? What new insights do you have about how you handle these stressors? What is the most relevant strategy learned in this lesson?*

Check for Understanding

Have students complete an exit ticket: *Why are internalizing and externalizing strategies considered "avoidance" coping? What role does emotion play in these actions? How can these approach strategies (problem solving and seeking social support) help a person make progress?*

Name:_____ Date: _____

PACT Problem Solving

Directions: Consider a problem and complete the flowchart using the PACT problem-solving strategy.

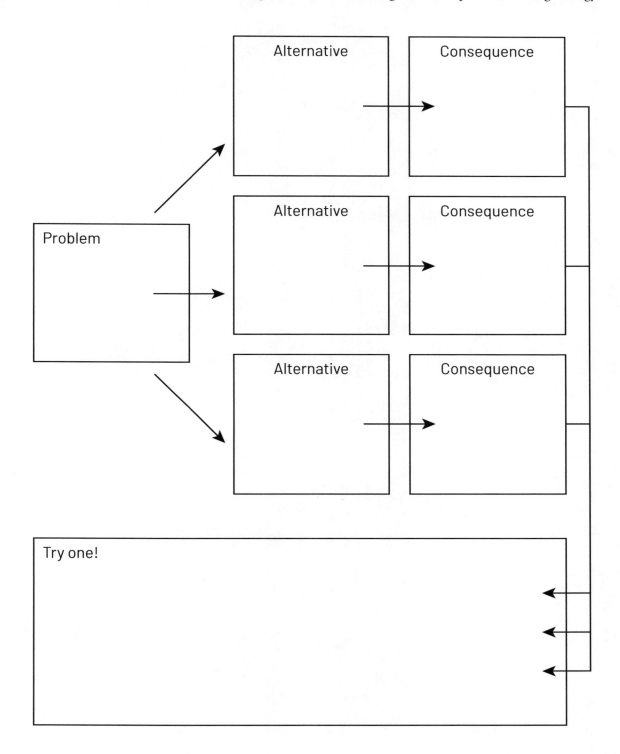

Can Stress Lead to Success?

Stress is inevitable, but instead of encouraging students to eliminate stress, we can help them "stress better" by guiding awareness of how stress is framed. In Bar-On's (2013) model, stress tolerance is the "ability to effectively and constructively manage emotions" (para. 30). It describes students' abilities to problem solve through stressful events using positive strategies instead of experiencing negative anxiety.

When stressors (e.g., a forthcoming test or a deadline on a big project) are responded to with negative perceptions of stress, this is known as *distress*. However, not all stress is distress. *Eustress* comes from the field of positive psychology (see Seligman & Csikszentmihalyi, 2000) and is known as positive stress. Oftentimes, students' appraisal of a situation determines if a stressor will lend itself to distress or eustress. For example, if a student has a big project due, there is opportunity for either type of stress. If the student feels well-equipped, competent, and confident that he can produce the project at his desired level of achievement, then eustress is likely. However, distress may develop if the student is having difficulty locating resources, collaborating with others, or finding time to finish the assignment. The student becomes anxious and frazzled, as he attempts to fulfill the assignment requirements without optimal resources.

Being aware of framing stress as eustress rather than distress can be new for many students who may not recognize that stress is not always negative. The goal is not to eliminate stress but to channel positive stress that will support performance. How do we support this change?

According to researchers such as Jamieson, Mendes, Blackstock, and Schmader (2010) and Brooks (2014), how people appraise or assess a task can make a difference in supporting the shift to eustress. Jamieson and colleagues found that when people were told that physiological signs of stress (e.g., increased heart rate and extra physical energy) predict stronger performance, they performed more strongly on high-stakes standardized tests. The participants reframed how they thought about the physiological signs of stress. Instead of thinking about their physical responses to stress as anxiety, participants understood them as functional.

Brooks (2014) studied how it is often difficult to move from a state of anxiety to a state of calm. Instead of moving to a state of calm, we can reframe our thinking about anxiety to a state of positive excitement, for both have similar physiological responses. Brooks found when people were told to verbally state "I am excited" three times prior to performance while smiling, they were able to improve their performance more than those who either stated, "I am anxious," or made no statement prior to performing. Those who said, "I am excited," were also more likely to interpret feelings of anxiety as excitement. The stress could be helpful for performance.

Psychologists Yerkes and Dodson (1908) examined the relationship between anxiety arousal and performance. They found that when stress was too high or too low, performance weakened. When stress is low, apathy is present. A student does not care about an easy spelling test and, thus, does not care about her performance on the test. On the other side, when stress is too high, performance suffers. We want our students to be between these poles, as students experiencing an optimal level of stress can exhibit high performance levels because they are sufficiently aroused and perceive that they have the resources to succeed with the task at hand.

In the end, we want students to be aware of their response to stress and appraise stress as a tool that gets them ready for a challenge ahead. During this lesson, focus your attention on the second and third rows of the Reframing Thinking Model (see Appendix). Emphasize that when students experience emotion related to stress, such as anxiety or fear, they can think about the stress as a threat or a challenge. If the thought is reframed as a challenge, then there is potential for emotions to be regulated to positive excitement. The reframing can help the student seek ways to regulate the stress (make a plan, seek support, etc.).

This lesson addresses stress related to pre-performance anxiety or typical, everyday stress. For students dealing with more chronic or clinical anxiety or trauma, it is important to address these issues with more focused, individualized interventions with appropriate professionals.

Big Idea

Can stress lead to success?

Objectives

Students will:

- be able to differentiate between types of stress,
- understand that the way we think about stress affects the way our body reacts to stress, and
- be able to apply techniques to reframe stress as a challenge rather than a threat.

Materials

- Image of "Eustress" graph (available online)
- Video: "How to Make Stress Your Friend" by Kelly McGonigal (available at https://www.ted.com/talks/kelly_mcgonigal_how_to_make_stress_your_friend)

Introduction

1. Ask students: *How would you define stress?* Explain that stress is emotional or mental strain due to demanding circumstances. Ask student to self-rate themselves about their level of stress: *How much stress have you experienced in the past year?* (None or little, average, a lot.)

2. Ask: *Do you think of stress as enhancing (it helps learning, motivation, productivity and health) or is stress debilitating (it hurts learning, motivation, productivity, and health)?* Explain to students that researchers have shown that if a person experiences "a lot" of stress during a year, they are more likely to die (about 42% increase in mortality when researchers studied more than 29,000 people; Keller et al., 2012). But this is only true if the person had a lot of stress *and* believed that stress is bad. These effects were not found among people who believed that stress is helpful.

3. Explain that this lesson will focus on understanding the "stress mindset." How we perceive stress actually affects how our bodies responds to stress. This is important because stress can be an obstacle we face in pursuit of long-term goals.

Class Activities

1. Ask students to complete a chart like Figure 9. Guide students to think about how they experience stress, specifically physical reactions, thoughts, and behaviors. Discuss responses.

2. Ask a few students to act out the following scenarios to show how they may respond to an upcoming performance. How might they act? What would their physical response be? What might their self-talk be?
   - A football player getting ready to play a football game.
   - A test-taker about to take a test.
   - A person who is about to sing karaoke in front of a large group.
   - A dancer who is about to perform a solo dance.

3. Ask: *What is similar about all of these experiences? What is different?* Explain to students that a professor (and former football player), Jeremy Jamieson, and colleagues (2010) thought it was interesting that football players would get really excited and amped up before a game but test-takers would get really nervous. They considered the physical reaction to the response to be similar and conducted a study where test-takers were told two different messages before taking a practice test. One group was told that stress can be good for you; it can help enhance performance. The other group was told to just focus. The group that was told that stress is enhancing did much better on practice tests (and later tests) than the group that was told just to focus.

4. Discuss the purposes of stress. Ask: *What happens to the human body when it experiences stress (e.g., sweaty palms, fast heartbeat, stomachache, inability to focus, fast breathing)? Why do you think this happens (i.e., the body is preparing for something that is perceived as a threat)? What would you say is the purpose of anxiety and stress (i.e., what they are telling us)?*

5. Review the following purposes for stress:
   - It can cause us to reach out to others for connection.
   - The stress channels chemicals into our bodies to help us survive (in a fight or flight response).
   - It can cause us to realize that something needs to change (in ourselves or lives) or cause us to be prepared for an upcoming challenge.

6. Provide the "label" for each purpose, as you continue to elaborate on these stress responses.
   - **Tend-and-befriend response:** Reaching out to ask for help or reaching out to help someone decreases fear and also increases courage. This stress

Stress feels like . . .	Stress looks like . . .
Stress sounds like . . .	Stress smells/tastes like . . .

FIGURE 9. The essence of stress sample chart.

motivates us to help the people we care about. The hormone oxytocin is released, increasing feelings of joy.

- **Fight-or-flight response:** Chemicals, such as adrenaline and cortisol, are released to help us survive the moment: This signals our body to leave immediately or fight for survival.
- **Challenge response:** This helps us rise to a challenge, such as taking a test, singing, playing football, or performing.

7. Explain that when something stressful happens, we can ask ourselves: Is this a *threat*, something that can hurt me (and those I care about), or is this a *challenge* I can face and overcome? If we perceive there are not enough resources to face the stressor, it is perceived as a threat. If we perceive that there are enough resources, the stress can be perceived as a *challenge* to overcome. Then, we can interpret physical reactions as a way to prepare our bodies for the challenge. Ask: *How might a person view an upcoming high-stakes test as a threat? How might a person view it as a challenge?*

8. Ask: *Do you think it would be a good idea to "calm down" and "relax" before a performance? Why or why not?* Explain that researchers have found that it is difficult to move from a state of anxiety to a state of calm. It is easier and more effective to move from anxiety to excitement. The physiological responses of anxiety are still present in the body, but the emotion is changed from negative to positive, which can be beneficial for performance.

9. Share these tips with students for dealing with stress or anxiety (especially associated with pre-performance anxiety):
- Say to yourself, "I have (physical reaction) in order to (get my body ready for the situation)." For example, "I have sweaty palms because my body is getting me ready for this challenge. My body is preparing me to *take*

action." (Refer students back to the purpose of challenge responses.) Or, "My heart is beating fast because I'm getting ready to face something big. I can do it!"

- ■ Say, "I'm excited, I'm excited, I'm excited!" Harvard researcher Alison Wood Brooks (2014) found that this is an effective way to reframe anxiety. This was found to increase performance on giving speeches, taking tests, and better karaoke singing, specifically the song, "Don't Stop Believing!" When you reframe your response as excitement, you think of the positive things that can happen in the next moment rather than become consumed by the performance outcome.

10. Tell students: *We can train to think like a football player thinks before a game— get amped up and excited. We can use the energy stress gives us. Not all stressful situations could or should be reframed positively, but some situations, such as being late, getting ready for a test, performing in front of others, are not life-or-death situations.*

11. Show students an image of the "eustress" graph. "Eustress" refers to a healthy kind of stress that is useful for preparing us for performance or challenge. Explain to students that it is important to be aware of when you are close to this zone or just outside of it. Being aware of physical reactions and how you frame challenges can help you get "in the zone" of eustress.

12. Ask students to draw a situation in which a performance-based stressful event is viewed as a threat versus a challenge (see Figure 10; guide students to choose something related to academic performance, athletic performance, etc., rather than something threatening such as war or fatal illness). Students should show how physical arousal stays the same, but the emotion changes from negative to positive.

13. Show the TED Talk: "How to Make Stress Your Friend." Ask: *How does this extend your understanding of what we have already learned? At the end she states, "Chasing meaning is better for your health than trying to avoid discomfort . . . go after whatever creates meaning in your life and then trust yourself to handle the stress that follows." What is your reaction to this quote? What would this mean for you in the next 24 hours . . . month . . . year . . . 10 years?*

Conclusion Connections

Connect the concept of eustress to other concepts studied in the unit (e.g., flow, obstacles, grit, growth mindset, approach coping vs. avoidance, etc.). Ask: *When stress is perceived as an obstacle or a threat, how does this affect our ability to tackle the obsta-*

SITUATION AS THREAT	SITUATION AS CHALLENGE
Include thought bubbles about the situation—viewing the situation as a threat.	Include thought bubbles about the situation—viewing the situation as a challenge.

FIGURE 10. Sample setup for student drawing.

cle? When stress is perceived as an opportunity or challenge, how does this affect how we approach the obstacle? How does the stress mindset relate to the concept of growth mindset?

Curriculum Extension

Have students read a summary or online article of Brooks's (2014) research on reframing anxiety as excitement or Jamieson et al.'s (2010) research on good stress (various articles are available online): *Why is our interpretation of stress important to developing a drive for excellence? How do our thoughts and beliefs about stress affect performance? What new insight does this article provide about the role of stress?*

Personal Reflection

Have students respond to the following: *What is your typical response to a challenge? Do you interpret academic challenges as threats or challenges? What tips from today's lesson will you most likely apply? How does stress positively and negatively affect your pursuit of excellence?*

Check for Understanding

Have students complete an exit ticket: *What is the purpose of stress? How does understanding its purpose help channel it effectively?*

From Procrastinating to Producing

When students wait until the last minute to submit or even begin a task, we may not be able to gauge their true levels of learning or progress. This intentional delay, or procrastination, can stifle or prevent student growth. But why do some students procrastinate?

There may be some emotional relief experienced through procrastination. Steel (2007) noted that if students are anxious about an impending activity, then students may be able to maintain a positive mood for a temporarily extended period by putting off the dreaded activity. But this hike in mood is short-lived; following procrastination, students' moods were less likely to be so rosy.

Some students may be anxious about not performing at a desired level on a task. They might feel they do not measure up or that they have to maintain the appearance of consistently performing at a particular level. The thought of producing something that is not up to specific expectations causes them internal pain, and the task is avoided. The student waits until the day before to study or begin a unit project. When the activity is assessed and the student earns a score that is not perfect, the blame can be passed on to the fact that little attention or resources were given to studying or creating the project. This allows the student to maintain an internal belief that he or she can do things perfectly; the outside factor of time led to the lack of perfect performance. Avoidance in the form of procrastination is one of several behaviors that may actually support the maintenance of perfectionism (Ramsey & Ramsey, 2002).

Regardless of the reason for procrastination, we have to support students to tackle and overcome it. But this can be difficult because it involves so much more than just time management; procrastination involves students' self-awareness, goal setting, decision making, and ways of thinking (Voge, 2007). When working with students who procrastinate, the strategies from the lesson on changing self-talk could be helpful (see Lesson 12). Also work with students to create personal goals. Deliberately teaching goal-setting strategies allows students to practice self-regulation skills (Grunschel, Patrzek, & Fries, 2013). When students learn to approach tasks by breaking them into smaller pieces, setting personal deadlines, and monitoring personal growth and progress, seemingly insurmountable tasks become achievable.

To prevent students from feeling overwhelmed and avoiding assignments, self-regulation strategies, including organization and goal setting, should be taught explicitly. For example, during a comprehensive project to demonstrate mastery over a large unit, a project timeline or calendar could be a part of each student's assignment. Here, students could be taught to begin with the due date of the project and work backward, setting mini-benchmarks. Teachers could model using a calendar and backward planning with a smaller assignment or test.

Students could also be taught to use if-then statements to reward themselves for meeting personal deadlines as a part of a larger project or assignment (e.g., "If I find all of my sources by Tuesday, then I will have time to hang out with my friends and watch a movie."). Small rewards, such as social time, can be attached to completing the current goal. The reward helps motivate the student to complete the mini-task. Students can suggest and choose appropriate awards, allowing more autonomy.

Finally, consider the mental contrasting approach with intentional implementation (WOOP; Oettingen, 2015), which can be used with any obstacle that inhibits progress toward a goal (see Lesson 5). Walking through each step of the process (i.e., envisioning the wish of accomplishing the task along with the positive outcomes and emotions associated with this achievement, envisioning the obstacle of procrastination as it stands in the way of the meeting the goal, and creating an if-then plan for when procrastination sneaks in) can help tackle procrastination with action.

Tips to share with students include:
- Do the easy parts first.
- Make a plan to the end with benchmarks along the way.
- Tell yourself to work for two more minutes before stopping.
- When stuck, ask for help.

Big Idea

Why procrastinate?

Objectives

Students will:
- be able to identify causes for procrastination, and
- be able to tackle procrastination through goal-setting strategies.

Materials

- Handout 17.1: Steps to Success

Introduction

Tell a few jokes about procrastination. Many are available online (e.g., "Me? A procrastinator? I'll prove you wrong one day!"). Ask: *Why do you think people procrastinate?*

Class Activities

1. Ask students to rate themselves on a scale from 1–5 how likely they are to do the following:
   - I put things off until the very last minute.
   - I am more likely to get it done if I wait until the last minute.
   - I usually tell myself, "I'll do it tomorrow."
   - When faced with a big project, I get overwhelmed thinking how to start.
   - If something is due soon, I often waste my time doing other things.

2. Explain to students that scores between 20 and 25 indicate that procrastination may be an issue for them. Say: *In order to understand procrastination, we have to be curious about our own behaviors. It's important to self-reflect and ask ourselves questions like, "What benefit do I get from putting things off? Why does putting something off provide more pleasant feelings than starting on it sooner?"* Then, ask: *What might the self-talk of a procrastinator be?* If students are willing to share, elicit responses.

3. Explain that human actions are based on what we *need* to do and what we *want* to do. People procrastinate because they either feel like they don't *need* to do something or they don't *want* to do it. For some procrastinators, the "need" motivation does not come until the feeling of panic takes over. The feeling of panic brings the "need" feeling to get a task done. Some people procrastinate as a way to "avoid" any negative feeling (like avoidance coping in Lesson 15). If the task is overwhelming, it evokes feelings of dread, frustration, or low confidence, and it is natural to want to avoid those feelings. Perfectionism often relates to procrastination. The feeling that "it has to be perfect" might cause a person to put off a task, to avoid unpleasant feelings associated with something not being good enough.

4. Share the following tips with students to overcome procrastination:
   - Take 5 minutes to make progress toward any task. Once something is started, our brains want to get back to the task and finish (this is called the Zeigarnik effect). Use the analogy of Swiss cheese—whenever something is unfinished (like holes in cheese), our brains want those holes to be filled.
   - Focus. Get rid of distractions. Dedicate a solid 15 minutes of uninterrupted time to the task. Put your phone away, don't allow yourself to check social media, and have all of your materials readily available. After you get used to 15 minutes of complete focused time, build up to 30 minutes, then 40, etc.
   - When you want to give up, push yourself to work for 2 more minutes. If you get stuck, ask for help.
   - Break big tasks down into smaller steps: We often get motivated by small triumphs, so breaking a task down into smaller ones can allow for these small moments of triumph and feelings of accomplishment.

5. Model how to break down a task into small goals using STEPs toward goals.
   - **Small:** Make sure the tasks are small and doable.
   - **Time:** Add a time element, such as when you will do the task or how long you will work on it.
   - **Energy:** Use the momentum of positive energy and motion to keep progressing.
   - **Progress:** Celebrate the progress you make.

6. Explain: *Let's say you have a project due in social studies next week. It involves researching a historical person and developing a PowerPoint presentation about his or her historical influence. This can be broken up into several steps:*
   - **Step 1:** Find resources.
   - **Step 2:** Read resources.

- **Step 3:** Take notes.
- **Step 4:** Make an outline.
- **Step 5:** Make a PowerPoint.
- **Step 6:** Add finishing touches (graphics, etc.).

7. Explain that each step is broken into smaller tasks that are more specific, and we can add a "time" element for each step (e.g., 30 minutes Thursday night for Step 1, 20 minutes Friday for Step 2, etc.). Positive emotions are evoked as progress is made.
8. Ask students to think of a long-term goal or project they have (personal, academic, extracurricular) and use Handout 17.1: Steps to Success to break the task into several small goals.
9. If procrastinators need motivation along the way, it is a good idea to celebrate small triumphs. Small rewards along the way might include a short break, ice cream, a quick check of social media, a break to read, etc.

Concluding Connections

Ask: *How does the idea "lean in and push through" relate to overcoming procrastination? How do emotions influence procrastination? How does this relate to the idea that "growth can be uncomfortable"?* Remind students that procrastination involves avoiding unpleasant emotion.

Curriculum Extension

Ask students to read an informational article about the Zeigarnik effect: *What is it? How was it discovered? What are the implications of the Zeigarnik effect beyond dealing with procrastination?*

Personal Reflection

Have students respond to the following: *In what situations are you most likely to procrastinate (academics, personal life, chores, practice, etc.)? What feelings are associated with procrastination? What is the motivation behind "avoiding" the task? What strategy from today's lesson seems most useful?*

Check for Understanding

Have students complete an exit ticket: *On a sticky note, write three tips for tackling procrastination that will inspire you the next time you want to put something off.*

Name: _____ Date: _____

Steps to Success

Directions: Write small goals and the time associated with each goal (amount of time or when to be done) on each step, leading toward your main goal at the top.

Main Goal:

_____

PART III

Guiding Emotion Toward Excellence

Big Idea

How can I use emotions so they work for me, not against me?

Big Ideas

- Self-awareness leads to self-management.
- Self-awareness catalyzes change.

LESSON	KEY QUESTION	CONCEPT(S)
Lesson 18: Understanding Emotions	What do emotions reveal?	Emotional self-awareness
Lesson 19: Managing Emotion	Do I control emotions, or do they control me?	Emotional self-awareness Impulse control
Lesson 20: Hope and Learned Optimism	How can I channel hope and optimism when faced with obstacles?	Optimism Adaptability
Lesson 21: Self-Awareness	How can self-awareness help me pursue excellence?	Emotional self-awareness
Lesson 22: A Matter of Perspective	Do you see what I see?	Reality testing Interpersonal skills

LESSON	KEY QUESTION	CONCEPT(S)
Lesson 23: Interpersonal Problem Solving	How can perspective-taking enhance relationships?	Problem solving Interpersonal skills
Lesson 24: Assuredly Assertive	How can I effectively communicate my thoughts, feelings, and needs?	Interpersonal skills Self-expression

Students' journeys to success will include many emotional highs and lows. Both students and educators should have an understanding of the emotional experiences that accompany achieving goals and facing obstacles so that emotion can be channeled to fuel the pursuit of excellence.

Bar-On's (2006) model of emotional intelligence is used as a framework for organizing many of the lessons. His model describes emotional and social intelligence, and specifically focuses on intrapersonal skills, interpersonal skills, stress management, adaptability, and general mood. We know that when students develop these areas, it improves their social, emotional, and academic endeavors. Students cannot actualize potential by focusing on academic skills alone; emotions are finely intertwined with academic and social success. Students must be emotionally smart, meaning that they must understand personal feelings and those of others in order to optimally thrive in all areas of life. Just as cognitive abilities and mindsets are malleable, emotional intelligence is malleable. Bar-On's (2013) model describes emotional intelligence as an array of interrelated emotional and social competencies, skills, and behaviors that impact intelligent behavior. Students with a limited understanding of emotions are not doomed to a life lacking in emotional awareness and power. Students can grow their emotional IQs. We can teach students about emotions and the effects of emotions on achievement and progress, demonstrating how emotions, thoughts, and behaviors impact each other, whether supporting or hindering progress. In this section, we share lessons that support students so that they can understand how to manage and use emotions to facilitate achievement. Students learn that self-awareness leads to self-management, and self-awareness catalyzes change.

Understanding Emotions

Emotions are not academic constructs and do not receive the attention or support that traditional curricular areas often maintain. Many theories of intelligence even leave emotions out of the equation. Yet, the growth and excellence that we desire for our students cannot happen without a firm understanding of the impact of emotions on thoughts and behaviors.

On the other hand, emotional self-awareness is included in almost every model of emotional intelligence. Bar-On (2013) defined self-awareness as our ability to be aware of, identify, and understand our emotions. Emotional self-awareness is important when considering paths to excellence because emotions are attached to the experiences that both inspire growth and impede performance. When students understand that they experience specific emotions in conjunction with behaviors or activities that support or detract from their goals, they can be aware of how emotions can help or hurt their progress toward goals. Unpleasant emotions that accompany setbacks are often not easy to stomach; it may be much more comfortable to avoid or gloss over highly emotional experiences. But, once again, this is a time for students to lean in and push through. If emotions are not dealt with in the present, they will eventually resurface later.

Goleman (2005) noted that self-awareness of our emotions allows us to more easily pilot our lives. There is a purpose for the positive emotions that accompany student interests. Those who have strong self-awareness have clarity regarding their strengths and what motivates them (Bradberry & Greaves, 2009). A student writer may enter a state of flow when creating the next part of her poem in progress; this is accompanied by positive emotions, which reinforce the behaviors surrounding both flow and the activity of interest. The positive emotions and feelings support continued progress. On the other hand, emotions can be additional challenges that students must overcome. Students experiencing maladaptive perfectionism or a fixed mindset may have feelings of fear or apprehension when approaching a challenging task. As a result, the challenging task and the accompanying emotions are avoided.

Students need to self-reflect on emotions as they relate to achievement motivation concepts, such as growth mindset, grit, tenacity, flow, and procrastination. When students begin to discuss and understand the emotions associated with each of these concepts, they can also begin to reflect on their own decisions and behaviors. They can consider how fear kept them from getting started on their history project or how joy supported a drive to independently learn more about marine biology. Without emotions, we would not experience the joy of learning something new in our areas of interest. Positive emotions fuel progress toward passion. When students begin to understand and connect personal emotions to behaviors, they have unlocked a powerful tool. They know what tasks will be motivating and what tasks will be difficult based upon known emotional patterns. And, as Goleman (2005) noted, this knowledge allows students to more effectively pilot their lives.

In this lesson, guide students to consider the role of emotions in pursuing excellence.

Big Idea

What do emotions reveal?

Objectives

Students will:
- analyze the purpose and need for emotions,
- analyze how emotions are related, and
- self-reflect on the complexities of emotions as they relate to achievement motivation concepts (e.g., growth mindset, grit, tenacity, etc.).

Materials

- Handout 18.1: Emotion Words (cut out in advance)
- Handout 18.2: Need for Emotion Chart
- Paint swatches (one for each student or pair of students)
- Image of Plutchik's Color Wheel of Emotion (available online)
- Video: "Emotions and the Brain" by Sentis (available at https://www.youtube.com/watch?v=xNY0AAUtH3g)

Introduction

1. Distribute cutouts from Handout 18.1: Emotion Words (if you don't want to cut them out, students may label the words as a part of a category or use a specific symbol to note a specific category). Ask students to sort the emotions into categories (you may have to clarify the definition of some emotions for students). Ask: *How did you organize these? What title would you give each category? Do some emotions belong in more than one category?*
2. Distribute paint swatches from a paint store or hardware store. Ask students to assign emotion words to each color (from their emotion words and/or adding their own words). For example, for various shades of red, they may assign varied levels of anger (e.g., irritated, aggravated, furious, enraged).
3. Ask students to share their responses, noting the various interpretations of degrees of emotion.

Class Activities

1. Show students Plutchik's Color Wheel of Emotion. Ask students to describe the organizational patterns of the emotions (e.g., organized by opposites, organized by level of intensity, organized by motivations, etc.). Ask students to choose one petal of the wheel (e.g., ecstasy, joy, serenity) and think of scenarios when a person's emotion would change on the spectrum. Plutchik claimed that there are eight basic emotions (joy, fear, trust, surprise, sadness, disgust, anger, anticipation) with various degrees, intensities, and combinations (Plutchik & Kellerman, 1980). Note that the wheel folds down to indicate more relationships.
2. Ask: *What is the relationship between awe and disapproval? How are they alike? What are some things you notice about how emotions are organized?*
3. Explain that all emotions have a purpose and are linked to a need. Distribute Handout 18.2: Need for Emotion Chart for students to complete. Guide discussion using Figure 11.
4. Explain that emotions are complex and often involve "blends" of emotions. Refer to Plutchik's Color Wheel of Emotion, and ask: *What emotions would be combined to form "jealousy"?* (Fear, sadness, and anger.) Ask students to also develop combinations for pride (anger + joy), love (joy + trust), despair (fear + sadness), hope (anticipation + trust), and curiosity (trust + surprise).
5. Ask: *Why is it important to understand your emotions, specifically their need and purpose? How do emotions influence a drive for excellence? How might they*

EMOTION	EXAMPLE EXPERIENCES	PURPOSE	NEED INDICATED
Fear/Anxiety	Student responses	To avoid threat, to protect	To be reassured
Anger	Student responses	To make change, to cause action, to release energy when faced with a threat	To be respected
Sadness	Student responses	To hide anger, to retreat, to deal with loss	To be comforted
Joy	Student responses	To share, to connect with others, to trust	To feel satisfaction
Regret	Student responses	To move us towards our goals	To feel hope

FIGURE 11. Teacher's guide to Handout 18.2.

divert your drive for excellence? How do emotions relate to concepts presented in other lessons? Review related concepts and talk with students about which emotions are associated with each (some from the color wheel, or otherwise). Emphasize that unpleasant emotions can be associated with positive concepts (e.g., being "gritty" may involve some unpleasant emotion). Many concepts involve both pleasant and unpleasant emotions.

- **Grit/tenacity:** Love, interest, optimism, joy, trust, acceptance, admiration, apprehension, discomfort
- **Flow:** Joy, trust, interest, optimism, awe
- **Growth mindset:** Trust, discomfort, apprehension, courage, facing fear
- **Fixed mindset:** Comfort, safety, fear of unknown
- **Perfectionism:** Remorse, disgust, fear, apprehension, pride, joy
- **Procrastination:** Temporary comfort; avoiding pain, annoyance, distraction, fear
- **Goal setting:** Optimism, trust, joy, anticipation

6. Ask: *Can we control emotions, or do they control us? Can you make yourself feel sad? Angry? Joyful? How do you do it?* (By thinking about something, by having a memory, etc.) Explain: *In our distracted, busy world, it can be difficult to be self-aware of our own emotions and how they influence our actions and behaviors, but we can manage emotions and use them for our benefit* (see Lesson 20

on optimism). *When we become self-aware of our emotions, we can be curious about ourselves and ask, "What is this emotion telling me? What is its purpose? Is this motivating me toward action?" This can help lead to management of emotions* (in future lessons). Follow this discussion with the video "Emotions and the Brain."

Conclusion Connections

1. Ask: *Why is it important to lean into and explore our emotions rather than try to push them aside or avoid them? Even when emotions are unpleasant, why is it important to "feel" them?* (Understanding what we feel and why brings the emotion to a conscious level so that we can move forward to manage the emotion.)
2. (Optional) Have students respond to the following in their journals: *Next time you feel an unpleasant emotion, ask yourself what the purpose of that emotion is and reflect on your need. Explore the emotion and what triggers your emotional response (past experiences, your values, memories) to a particular situation.*

Curriculum Extensions

Have students complete one or more of the following:
- View a piece of art, such as *The Subway* by George Tooker (1950): What emotions are evoked? What emotions are revealed? How does the artist produce this effect? How do the emotions relate to the ideas portrayed in the art? Use Plutchik's color wheel or modified versions of it to name the emotions.
- Read a speech such as "Day of Infamy" by Franklin D. Roosevelt, "I Have a Dream" by Martin Luther King, Jr., or "The Space Shuttle Challenger Address" by Ronald Reagan: Use Plutchik's color wheel to identify the emotions that the speech writer evokes in the audience. How did the authors achieve this emotional effect?
- Conduct an emotional ups-and-downs analysis for a character in a specific short story or novel. Create a line graph showing ups and downs of the character's emotions and levels of intensities. Refer to Plutchik's color wheel and consider combined emotions as well.

Personal Reflection

Have students respond to the following: *Create an emotion line graph to show the emotions you experience within a day (or possibly week). Time can be the x-axis, and type of emotion (positive/negative) can be the y-axis. Include times when you may experience more than one emotion at once (happy and sad at the same time). What insight do you have about yourself from this graph? How does this graph relate to the ideas of grit, growth mindset, sticking to a goal, flow, pursuing excellence, etc.?*

Check for Understanding

Have students complete an exit ticket: *How can understanding emotion be helpful in pursuing excellence?*

HANDOUT 18.1
Emotion Words

Directions: Sort the emotions into categories.

Optimism	Interest	Aggressiveness
Annoyance	Contempt	Remorse
Boredom	Disgust	Disapproval
Pensiveness	Distraction	Awe
Appreciation	Submission	Love
Serenity	Acceptance	Anger
Sadness	Surprise	Fear
Joy	Trust	Ecstasy
Rage	Vigilance	Anticipation
Loathing	Amazement	Grief
Terror	Admiration	

Name:_____ Date: _____

Need for Emotion Chart

Directions: Reflect on situations in which you experienced each of the emotions in the chart. Then, think about the purpose and indicated need of each emotion.

EMOTION	EXAMPLE EXPERIENCES	PURPOSE	NEED INDICATED
Fear/Anxiety	*Feeling before giving a speech in front of a large audience.*	*To avoid threat, to protect.*	*To be reassured.*
Anger			
Sadness			
Joy			
Regret			

Managing Emotion

O ne component of Bar-On's (2006) model of emotional intelligence focuses on the ability to manage and control emotions so that they work for us and not against us. Once students are self-aware of emotions, they can feel empowered to use emotions to support growth and resilience.

We oftentimes do not have control over when we will be impacted by emotions or even what the emotions will be, but we do have the capability to manage the duration of and associated behaviors that come with emotions (Goleman, 2005). Students may not have control over getting rejected from the varsity team. They may also not have control over the disappointment that follows. However, when students are self-aware of their emotions, this brings a sense of control, and the trajectory of disappointment can be managed. Goleman suggested that the rejected students try an activity that distracts them from the pain of disappointment: Play a video game, call a friend, or watch a funny movie. These mood-shifting distractions are powerful and allow students to move on from the negative emotional state and get back on a road to goals and progress.

Emotional management is evident when individuals are able to put momentary needs on hold in order to pursue greater goals (Bradberry & Greaves, 2009). For students, this means that they can choose how they respond to situations instead of allowing emotions to choose for them. As an example, just before going on stage at the school play, a student's younger sibling drops the student's new phone, shattering the screen. The student wants to speak to the younger sibling in anger. However, if the student has developed a level of emotional management, then the student may be able to put the immediate emotional need of anger on hold and swiftly change gears to skillfully perform in the play. A strong performance in the play does not mean that the student is not upset. But the student is able to take control of the situation and switch gears in a way that allows the larger goal to be executed even in a potentially contentious moment. Self-management is the ability to use emotional awareness to stay flexible and positively direct behavior (Bradberry & Greaves, 2009). The student has not forgotten about the sibling's mishap, but the student is emotionally strong enough to flexibly switch or support emotions when needed to maintain progress. As students continue to grow their abilities to manage emotions, they will also learn more about their personal triggers and causes of particular emotions; this knowledge equips students to consider how emotional reactions impact behavior and progress.

When students are able to analyze and manage emotions, they move toward mindful excellence, aware of how their thoughts, emotions, and beliefs about abilities affect how they pursue developing potential. Students can consider whether they can control emotions or if emotions control them, especially during stressful situations, such as taking algebra for high school credit. They comprehend the cognitive, physical, and social impacts stemming from the associated emotions. In this situation, connected elements may include increased heart rate when going to schedule classes, displaying anger to others when asked about classes, and, perhaps, avoidance of the course. When students understand the connections and potential ripple effects of emotions on behaviors, relationships, and one's pursuit of excellence, mindful excellence can begin to take shape. Students can weigh elements beyond the tangible behaviors; they can think through the emotional possibilities before they happen. This is powerful. Emotions are no longer in the driver's seat. Instead, we are teaching students how to steer and change lanes on their own.

During this lesson, remind students of the concept of "lean in and push through." You may also refer to the Reframing Thinking Model (see Appendix), specifically the last row. Emphasize that it is important to bring awareness of emotion to our thinking so that we can be thoughtful in how we respond or cope with that emotion. Self-awareness catalyzes change.

Big Idea

Do I control emotions, or do they control me?

Objectives

Students will:
- reflect on causes and specific triggers for given emotions;
- forecast "ripple effects" of emotions on behaviors, relationships, and one's pursuit of excellence; and
- practice applying various techniques to manage emotion.

Materials

- Handout 18.1: Emotion Words
- Handout 19.1: Emotions and Experiences
- Handout 19.2: Ripple Effect of Emotions
- Handout 19.3: Emotional Toolbox
- *The Mixed-Up Chameleon* by Eric Carle
- Chart Paper (one piece per group of 2–3 students)
- (Optional) Video: "Your Body Language May Shape Who You Are" by Amy Cuddy (available at https://www.ted.com/talks/amy_cuddy_your_body_language_shapes_who_you_are)

Introduction

1. Share with students a definition of emotional intelligence: "Emotional intelligence includes emotional and social skills and behaviors that influence intelligent behavior" (Bar-On, 2013, para. 1). Ask: *Do you think emotional intelligence is malleable, or do you think people are just born with these abilities (e.g., are you born a pessimist?)?* Explain that like growth mindset, emotional intelligence can also be developed. Although people are born with different temperaments, we can still improve our abilities to handle emotions like fear, anger, and even joy and optimism.

2. Distribute cutouts from Handout 18.1. Using the same words, ask groups of 2–3 students to create a linear continuum of emotion from worst feeling (bottom) to best feeling (top). Allow students to experiment with developing the continuum. Ask students to share their responses and reflect.

Class Activities

1. Read aloud *The Mixed-Up Chameleon* by Eric Carle. Ask: *What lesson does this book teach about the emotion of happiness? Did the circumstances determine happiness?* (*Note.* The chameleon got everything he wanted, but he was still not happy. Guide students to understand that as he became self-aware that he was not happy, he changed his outlook and actions.)

2. Ask students to use their continuums of emotions to trace the ups and downs of emotion experienced by the chameleon. Ask: *In what ways did the chame-*

leon attempt to seek relief from his unpleasant emotions? (He was bored and felt relief by seeking contentment, but he became frustrated, disappointed, and perhaps even worried. These emotions were relieved by positive expectation and eventually appreciation of being himself as a chameleon.)

3. Explain that self-awareness of emotion is necessary for self-management of emotion. When we feel an emotion, we can lean into the emotion and remember its purpose and the need it reflects: *Emotions are controlled by our limbic system. It often seems that we have no control over how we feel. However, when we become aware of our emotions, we get to have control over them again. Our emotions are related to memories, values, and experiences. Understanding your triggers and how they relate to your memories, values, and experiences can help you control your emotions.*

4. **Understanding triggers:** Distribute Handout 19.1: Emotions and Experiences. Ask students to associate memories, values, and experiences with each emotion as well as specific triggers that might incite the emotion. Note that this is a personal reflection and students need not share responses with the group. Use Figure 12 to guide discussion. Ask: *Why is it important to be aware of experiences that incite specific emotions in us?* (Awareness helps us understand triggers. Understanding triggers can help us prepare for situations in which we can manage our emotions.)

5. **Knowing the ripple effects of emotion:** Assign groups of 2–3 students one of the following emotions: fear, despair, jealousy, insecurity, anger, disappointment, pessimism, optimism, joy. Using chart paper or Handout 19.2: Ripple Effect of Emotions, ask students to complete a ripple effect for a given emotion, showing physical reactions of the body (heart racing, body language, gestures) when the emotion might be experienced, behaviors that are likely to happen because of that emotion, how the emotional reaction could affect relationships with other people, and how it relates to pursuing excellence. (Note that individuals experience emotions differently, so group members may have varied responses in the ripples.) Afterward, hold a gallery walk in which students add ideas as they rotate through the group stations. Ask: *Why is it important to be self-aware of ripple effects? What kind of ripples do you want to create* (Bradberry & Greaves, 2009)? Figure 13 may be helpful to guide students.

6. **Regulating intensity of emotion:** Ask: *What are some negative consequences of uncontrolled emotions?* When uncontrolled negative emotions become intense, they may lead to negative interactions with others, or embarrassment. Discuss Handout 19.3: Emotional Toolbox and ways to control the intensity of a feeling or emotion. Explain that it is not necessarily "wrong" to experience an unpleasant emotion, but it is important to be aware of the

EMOTION	EXPERIENCE (ASSOCIATED MEMORY, PERSONAL VALUES, EXPERIENCES)
Sadness	Death of grandmother, not winning game, saying good-bye to friends
Fear/Anxiety	Home flooding, childhood monsters under the bed, getting on an airplane, taking math tests
Happiness	Birthday party, travel experience, community service
Jealousy	A friend receives special recognition
Disappointment	Being left out of friend group, not being accepted as part of a group
Anger	Being treated unfairly, someone stealing something from me, someone being mean to me
Hopefulness	Getting a second chance when it was not deserved, figuring out a different way to do something

FIGURE 12. Teacher's guide to Handout 19.1.

purpose of the emotion and what it is motivating or preparing us to do (e.g., tackling a challenge).

7. Then, ask students to circle the top 3–4 strategies on Handout 19.3 that they would use to regulate intense emotions. Explain that intense unpleasant emotions are only temporary; the painful "sting" of the emotion lasts about 90 seconds (Taylor, 2009). Emotional discomfort can build emotional strength. It is better to endure the sting than shove the emotion aside or distract yourself from feeling the pain altogether. The feeling will linger, but will subside in intensity. A student can get through the other side of the sting with "next steps" and a plan to move forward, making progress even *through* the crying, fear, or despair. The emotional strength comes from leaning into the discomfort and pushing through it.

8. Guide students to understand how intense emotions can be regulated through coping strategies (e.g., intense anger could be regulated by deep breathing). Refer back to Plutchik's Color Wheel of Emotion and continuums from earlier in the lesson. Ask students to think about how feeling overwhelmed might be dealt with and what the resulting feeling would be. Then, guide students through other emotions (disappointment, anxiety, jealousy, etc.).

9. **(Optional) Using body language for positive emotion:** Explain that researchers have found that our physical posture and body language can actually influence how we feel (e.g., when people place a pen in their mouths, the

EMOTION	PHYSICAL RESPONSES	BEHAVIOR	EFFECTS ON OTHER PEOPLE	EFFECT ON PURSUIT OF EXCELLENCE
Fear (or anxiety)	Increased heart rate, sweaty palms, shallow breathing	May lead to anger response or avoiding of experiences	People may feel they need to comfort you	Avoidance of challenging tasks
Despair	Skipped heartbeat, crying, deep breaths	May blame other people for problems, may reach out for support	People may encourage you	Too afraid or discouraged to get out of comfort zone
Jealousy	May create reaction of fear; increased adrenaline	Can lead to aggression (wanting other person to feel hurt)	May lead to unstable relationships or broken relationships	May be difficult to work with others who are at your competitive level
Insecurity	Crying due to self-doubt; acting out aggressively toward others	May overcompensate or belittle others (want to feel more successful than others)	May hurt others' feelings, make others feel belittled	May not be willing to take risks
Anger	Increased heart rate Aggressive body language	May make rash statements or act out with yelling	May lead to unnecessary negativity in relationships, damaged relationships	May not get to focus on goals; distracted by the strong emotion
Disappointment	Sinking heart, crying	May avoid social interactions, may seek out support	Lose contact with others, need opportunities to share with others	Too discouraged to keep pursuing forward toward excellence

FIGURE 13. Sample ripple effects.

EMOTION	PHYSICAL RESPONSES	BEHAVIOR	EFFECTS ON OTHER PEOPLE	EFFECT ON PURSUIT OF EXCELLENCE
Pessimism	Closed body language (crossed arms)	Consistently negative when talking to others; expects the worst in situations, avoids situations	May bring others down with negativity	May be easily discouraged by an obstacle; might not want to keep going after an obstacle
Optimism	Smiles, open body language	Expects good outcomes, tries new things	Attracts others, positive impact on relationships	May energize one toward achieving a goal; a setback will be seen as temporary, so they will work through it
Joy	Smile, open body language, increased heart rate	Visible positivity, sociable, complimentary	Supports positive emotions in others	May energize a person to keep going; will gain satisfaction from their work

FIGURE 13. Continued.

muscles that create a smile actually lift one's mood). Show the video "Your Body Language May Shape Who You Are" by Amy Cuddy. She discusses how the "power pose" can help anyone with insecurity or lack of confidence face challenges or intimidating experiences with strength and courage. (*Note*. There has been some controversy on whether Cuddy's findings are replicable, specifically in increasing hormone levels. Nevertheless, there have been consistent results in perceived benefits, which is overall helpful.)

Conclusion Connections

Ask students: *How can managing emotion help you as you face difficult tasks . . . as you face uncertainty . . . as you face intimidating situations . . . as you experience disappointment from setbacks . . . as you face the fear of failure? How does managing emotion relate to the idea of mindful excellence?*

Curriculum Extensions

Have students complete one or more of the following:
- In a short written response, analyze a character from a short story or novel: What does the character do to try to manage unpleasant emotions? Does he or she use positive strategies or negative ones? How does the character's approach to managing his or her emotions affect his or her relationships with other characters?
- Research more about how emotion is processed in the brain. Which parts of the brain process emotion, and how do they interact? Develop a presentation to share your findings.

Personal Reflection

Have students respond to the following: *What are your personal triggers for unpleasant emotions? From the strategies discussed today, what are your top three go-to strategies to positively manage your emotions? What new strategy might you try?*

Check for Understanding

Have students complete an exit ticket: *Why is it important to become self-aware of triggers for our emotions? Why is it important to be self-aware of how our emotions affect us and others? What "control" do you have over your emotions?*

Name: _____ Date: _____

Emotion and Experiences

Directions: What experiences are associated with each emotion? How might your awareness of these memories and experiences help promote management of emotion?

EMOTION	EXPERIENCE (ASSOCIATED MEMORY, PERSONAL VALUES, EXPERIENCES)
Sadness	
Fear/Anxiety	
Happiness	
Jealousy	
Disappointment	
Anger	
Hopefulness	

Name:_____ Date:_____

HANDOUT 19.2
Ripple Effect of Emotions

Directions: Complete a ripple effect for a given emotion, showing physical reactions of the body (heart racing, body language, gestures) when the emotion is experienced, behaviors that are likely to happen from that emotion, how the emotional reaction affects relationships with other people, and how it relates to pursuing excellence.

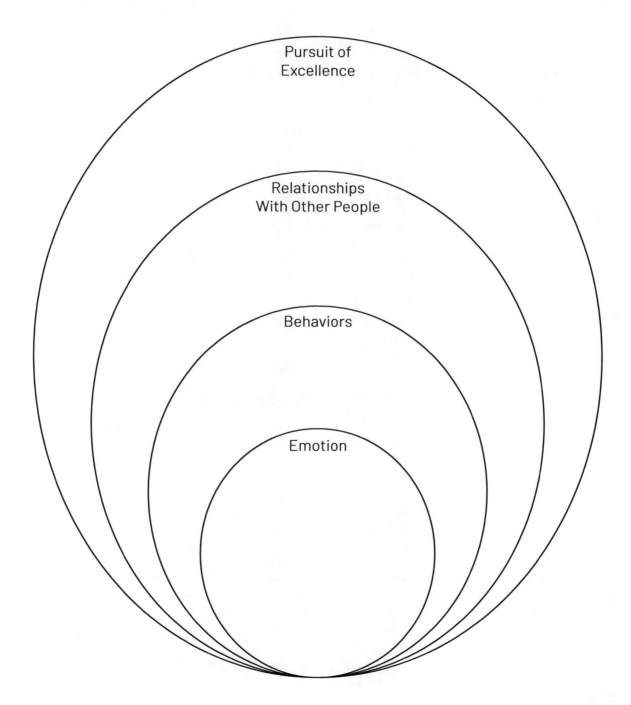

Name:_____ Date: _____

Emotional Toolbox

Directions: Review the following ways to control the intensity of a feeling or emotion.

1. Take deep breaths and even close your eyes when feeling overwhelmed, stressed, frustrated, or angry.

2. Pause 5 seconds before speaking, especially if angry.

3. If anxious, to calm down, take deep breaths to allow oxygen to get to your brain. To remain in a positive high-energy state say, "I'm excited!" three times.

4. When angry or upset, imagine putting a filter over your mouth before you speak.

5. Change your facial expression (researchers have indicated that smiling can actually create a positive mood. Even just holding a pen in your mouth to make your muscles form a smile can lift mood).

6. Distract yourself for a short time until emotions calm down (take a walk, take a break).

7. Talk to a friend. Hearing someone else's opinion helps you see a broader perspective.

8. See the situation objectively, with no emotions attached. Imagine you see yourself from the perspective of a fly on the wall. See yourself with no negative judgment. Focus on one small step to move forward.

9. See the bigger picture: If emotionally upset, consider if the situation will be a big deal 5 years from now, 10 years from now, etc.

10. Exercise. It releases physical endorphins to help you feel happy.

11. Gratitude. Think of things you are thankful for. Keep a list.

12. Practice mindfulness. Take a few moments to be aware of the present, focusing your attention on each of your senses. What do you hear? Pay attention to your physical responses, your breathing, your heartbeat. What do you notice about your surroundings? (extend with taste, touch, etc.)

13. Do something kind for others. Doing something constructive to help others will shift the focus beyond yourself and will likely lift your mood.

14. Understand that the sting of an intense unpleasant emotion (anger, fear) is only temporary, usually 90 seconds. Although unpleasant emotions will still linger, unpleasant feelings are intense for only a short time. Endure the 90 seconds and know that it won't last forever. Getting through the initial sting of unpleasant emotion will build emotional strength, and you will know that you can get stronger through the experience.

Hope and Learned Optimism

Look on the bright side. Find the silver lining. Be positive. We perpetuate these sayings, but do they matter? Bar-On (2013) defined optimism as the ability to maintain a positive and hopeful attitude toward life even in the face of adversity. Seligman (2006) noted that without optimism achievement may not happen. Optimism facilitates the development of emotional intelligence and, further, desired achievement. Students who are optimists perceive that they can conquer challenges and more readily bounce back when they do not immediately achieve, making it more likely that they will try again and succeed.

Optimism is malleable; it can be learned and shaped. Learned optimism involves more than looking on the sunny side of life. Seligman (2006) conceptualized it as a set of cognitive skills that promotes resilience and flexibility. Learned optimism allows us to reattribute our negative pessimistic explanations for more optimistic causes. Suppose we get lost trying to find the pool at the hotel: We could say that our friend gave us bad directions (negative). On the other hand, we could say that we may have missed a turn. Neither explanation changes the current state (that we are lost), but the second explanation allows for change and ownership. According to Seligman, pessimistic thinking is escapable by learning and practicing cognitive skills that enable us to take charge and accomplish more through the ABCDE strategy:

- **Adversity:** Be aware of the adversity. What is the event that might trigger pessimistic thinking? *I just blew that exam!*
- **Belief:** This is how the adversity is interpreted because of a person's beliefs. Seligman cautioned us to separate our thoughts from our feelings at this stage. *Why do I believe that I did not do well on the exam? I am just not as smart as people think I am.*

- **Consequences:** This is how students act and feel as a result. Students must be aware of the consequences brought on by the adversity. *I feel shame and disappointment from this experience.*
- **Disputation:** This is where students reframe and change thoughts and beliefs. You want to interrupt the typical, negative thought pattern regarding the adversity and beliefs surrounding it to make them more rational and proactive. *I am not happy that I did not excel on the math exam as I wanted, but this is just one exam; one performance does not indicate my value as a person. I am still a smart person; this is just one mistake.*
- **Energization:** This is what happens next; the outcome of reframing and changing thoughts and beliefs. *I can review what and how I studied to see how I can improve for next time. I want to master more of the concepts and know that I can.*

Optimism's cousin is hope, believing you have both the will and the way to accomplish your goals (Goleman, 2005). Hopeful students perceive that they have the motivation, skills, and resources to achieve their goals. They consider methods for pushing through or moving beyond obstacles. Snyder and colleagues (2002) studied how hope interacted with intellectual aptitude and academic achievement among college students: Students of equivalent intelligence who attained different levels of academic achievement differed in their levels of hope. Hope was a better predictor of academic achievement than the often-used SAT scores. Students with more hope set higher goals and knew how to work hard to achieve them; they knew that problem solving, strategy, and effort could help them progress. Hope feeds off of optimism; if students have developed the skill of learned optimism, then students' cognitions will also set them up to have the positive motivational state of hope. This will be based on a sense of successful goal-directed energy and knowing multiple alternative ways to plan a method for reaching goals.

Together, optimism and hope also promote self-efficacy and adaptability. Self-efficacy is the perception that one has control of what is happening in one's life and that one can conquer challenges as they arise (Goleman, 2005). Self-efficacy is rooted in competency. If students feel capable, they will be more confident and willing to set higher goals. Instead of burying oneself after a setback, a student will consider a different approach.

During this lesson, continue to emphasize the Reframing Thinking Model (see Appendix), specifically the first column, working down (what is the situation, what is the thought, what is the emotion?). Lead students through the questioning of the thought (second row). Continually remind students about mindful excellence.

Big Idea

How can I channel hope and optimism when faced with obstacles?

Objectives

Students will:
- compare and contrast hope to optimism,
- apply elements of learned optimism to given situations, and
- understand that gratitude increases positive emotion and apply practices of gratitude.

Materials

- Handout 20:1: Change My Thinking
- "Dreams" by Langston Hughes and "Hope Is the Thing With Feathers" by Emily Dickinson
- Chart paper and markers for each small group

Introduction

Assign one of the quotes from Figure 14 to groups of 2–3 students. Ask groups to write the quote on chart paper and create an illustration to support the quote or think of examples to support the quote. Then, ask groups (staying together) to rotate to the other group papers (in a gallery walk) and add additional examples, symbols, and ideas. After all groups have rotated through, ask: *What concepts or ideas are represented by these quotes?* Elicit responses, guiding students to see hope, resilience, persistence, and optimism.

Class Activities

1. Ask students to develop definitions for *hope* and *optimism*. How are these concepts the same? How are they different? Then, share the following definitions from famous psychologists:

Hope is a waking dream.—Aristotle

If we are to achieve a victorious standard of living today, we must look for the opportunity in every difficulty instead of being paralyzed at the thought of the difficulty in every opportunity.—Walter E. Cole

If you hear a voice within you say "you cannot paint," then by all means paint and that voice will be silenced.—Vincent Van Gogh

Your present circumstances don't determine where you can go; they merely determine where you start.—Nido Qubein

I have been impressed with the urgency of doing. Knowing is not enough; we must apply. Being willing is not enough; we must do.—Leonardo da Vinci

I have learned over the years that when one's mind is made up, this diminishes fear.—Rosa Parks

The only person you are destined to become is the person you decide to be.—Ralph Waldo Emerson

FIGURE 14. Quotes about hope, resilience, persistence, and optimism.

- **Hope:** A positive motivational state based on a sense of successful goal-directed energy and ways to plan out meeting goals. People with hope see barriers as challenges to overcome and can think of multiple pathways to attain their goals (Snyder, 2000).
- **Learned optimism:** The idea that joy can be developed. Optimists view failure as temporary instead of permanent. They feel empowered to conquer the challenge before them. They don't think that one bad event will generalize to other events (one bad moment in the morning does not mean the entire day will be bad). Pessimists feel helpless and feel that the obstacle is a permanent setback. One specific bad event translates into interpreting other nonrelated events as negative (Seligman, 2006).

2. **Mental contrasting (WOOP):** Revisit mental contrasting, specifically the WOOP strategy from Lesson 5. Remind students that successful people achieve goals not by simply being positive, happy, and oblivious to problems. They have a slightly pessimistic perspective—think of what might happen if you have an obstacle. The "contrast" in thinking about both the positive outcome and a negative obstacle motivates them to tackle the obstacle. Emphasize hope. Multiple plans can be made for obstacles (i.e., if-then

plans); there is a will and a way to move forward. Ask students how they have applied this strategy since it was introduced.

3. **Changing thinking:** Learned optimism involves thinking about beliefs and disputing them. (*Note.* This is the SWAT strategy from Lesson 12 but goes beyond "should/worry" thoughts.) If you notice that a particular situation triggers a strong emotion (fear, despair, anger, pessimism), then bring into awareness the thoughts you have that are influencing that emotion. Then, challenge those thoughts with logical reasoning. Guide students through Handout 20.1: Change My Thinking (see Figure 15 for examples). In challenging a thought, there are elements of hope—making a plan to change, to take control of the situation, and to see the setback as temporary. This exercise is a way to condition oneself toward optimism. Emphasize acknowledging the feeling, leaning into the discomfort, and providing positive self-talk to move through the emotion.

4. **Attitude of gratitude:** Explain that an attitude of gratitude produces positive emotion. Ask students to make a list of 100 things they are thankful for with specific details. They should consider moments, people, and memories (e.g., being thankful for the special moment with my grandmother before she died, for the cool breeze blowing on my face, etc.). Ask students to consider keeping a gratitude journal and adding 5–10 things to their list daily.

5. **Walk of thank yous:** When feeling overwhelmed with negative emotion, it can also be helpful to take a 5-minute walk and think about the things one is thankful for, including small details. Consider allowing gratitude walk during class time.

6. Read aloud "Dreams" by Langston Hughes. Ask the following questions in whole- or small-group discussion:
   - How is a dead dream like a broken-winged bird that cannot fly? How is a dead dream like a barren field frozen with snow?
   - What feelings are evoked in the poem? How is this achieved?
   - Does this poem relate more to hope or optimism?
   - How would an optimist view the meaning of this poem? How would a pessimist interpret it? (Use Seligman's definitions).

7. Read aloud "Hope Is the Thing With Feathers" by Emily Dickinson. Ask:
   - What obstacles are mentioned in the poem?
   - How is hope like a bird?
   - What does this poem reveal about perseverance?

SITUATION	THOUGHT/ BELIEFS	EMOTION	CHALLENGE THE THOUGHT
Getting a bad grade.	I'm not smart enough to do this.	Disappointment	This is just one assignment. This is not the end of the world. I can figure out what I did wrong and try to get better.
Things are not going your way while working on a group project.	These people are not responsible. I'm the only one who can do this right.	Frustration	Maybe my group members are confused. Maybe I can remind everyone of our goal, and we can divide the work into parts.

FIGURE 15. Sample responses to Handout 20.1.

Conclusion Connections

Ask: *How does this lesson relate to the idea of mindful excellence? How do our beliefs about setbacks (temporary vs. permanent) affect the pursuit of excellence? In what ways is discomfort associated with hope and optimism?*

Curriculum Extension

Have students read "Fragment 7: When Hope but made Tranquility be felt" by Samuel Taylor Coleridge: *What comparisons can you make with "Hope Is the Thing With Feathers" by Emily Dickinson? Create a Venn diagram to show the similarities and differences for how hope is described in each poem. Comment on the extent to which the poems' definitions relate to the definition of hope applied in this lesson.*

Personal Reflection

Have students respond to the following: *Do you consider yourself as seeing obstacles as permanent or temporary? How can questioning your thinking lead to more positive feelings? Think of a situation in which you viewed the issue in a negative light. Apply the "Change My Thinking" model to the situation. What was the challenge? What were your beliefs? What were your feelings? How might you dispute those beliefs?*

Check for Understanding

Have students complete an exit ticket: *Suppose someone said, "All you have to do is think positively, and you can achieve your dreams!" Is this true? Use what you have learned about hope and optimism to explain your answer.*

HANDOUT 20.1

Change My Thinking

Directions: Complete the chart. Think about any negative thoughts and emotions that might relate to the situation provided. Then, challenge the thought. Think of your own example for the last row.

SITUATION	THOUGHTS/ BELIEFS	EMOTION	CHALLENGE THE THOUGHT
Getting a bad grade.	*I'm not smart enough to do this.*	*Disappointment*	*This is just one assignment. This is not the end of the world. I can figure out what I did wrong and try to get better.*
Things are not going your way while working on a group project.			
Your own example:			

Teaching Tenacity, Resilience, and a Drive for Excellence © Prufrock Press Inc.

Self-Awareness

Know thyself. In Bar-On's (2013) model, emotional self-awareness is described as our ability to be aware of, identify, and understand our emotions. Beyond recognizing a particular emotion (e.g., anger vs. fear), self-awareness involves knowing why we feel a certain way and realizing the triggers that lead us to these feelings. Bar-On noted that self-awareness is included in every description, assessment, and definition of emotional intelligence; it is essential.

The Johari Window is a model that can be used to teach and improve self-awareness and mutual understanding among individuals and groups. Joseph Luft and Harry Ingham ("Jo-Hari"; 1955) developed the Johari Window model to promote understanding and training of self-awareness, personal development, and interpersonal relationships. The Johari Window features four quadrants that showcase information—feelings, attitudes, skills, motivations—within or about an individual person in relation to his or her group, from four perspectives:

1. **Open Area:** What an individual knows about self that is *also* known by others. We want students' Open Areas to grow. Here, they are self-aware and known by others. Students know what makes them stronger, and peers are aware of this and can offer support. When the Open Area is not developed, the student cannot share her strengths; they are unknown to both herself and her peers. Communication and feedback can foster growth in the Open Area, but students must be ready to accept feedback for growth.

2. **Blind Area:** What the individual does not know about self *but* others know. This is our personal blind spot. When students seek feedback, they learn what others see. A student may not be aware of his motivations, emotional triggers, and behaviors. Exploring the blind spot can help a student grow and develop both personal and academic skills. Perhaps a student is working on a speech but is unaware that she is using a monotone voice throughout

it. When practicing with a peer, the peer records her and suggests that her speech could be even stronger if she used more inflection. This student can grow in self-awareness and, perhaps, move this into the Open Area, as she is now more aware of her monotone tendency. Additionally, we help students explore the Blind Area by pointing out strengths or talents students may not know they have.

3. **Hidden Area:** What an individual knows about self that *others do not know*. The Hidden Area holds information that students know about themselves but have not shared with others; students may be shielding others from knowing how they really feel or act. Students have to become comfortable with disclosure in order to reduce the Hidden Area. This can be hard; this is a risk. What if my friends don't like me once they find out that . . . ? Students want to feel valued and may fear judgment. We have to create a culture of acceptance and openness so that students feel comfortable taking small risks and expressing their true selves. This area will be smaller in friend-friend relationships when compared to acquaintance relationships.

4. **Unknown Area:** What is unknown about self by both the individual *and* others. This includes aspects of our future—we don't know what our relationships might be in 10 years; we may not know how we would react to a situation (going to college) until it happens. This area also includes untapped skills or abilities; a student may not know that he has potential to be a great writer until there is an opportunity to develop those skills. This quadrant could also contain emotions that are unknowingly connected to particular experiences. A student may be unaware that his anger surrounding his broken family is impacting his peer relationships. At the same time, the students' peers might not understand the student's presented emotions. Self-discovery, feedback, and disclosure are key in this quadrant.

Big Idea

How can self-awareness help me pursue excellence?

Objectives

Students will:

- develop self-awareness about themselves and how others perceive them,
- analyze the impact of self-awareness on interpersonal relationships, and
- explore hidden aspects of themselves by planning new experiences.

Materials

- Handout 21.1: Johari Window
- Johari Adjectives List (accessible online)

Introduction

Explain that self-awareness is having an understanding of yourself and how others perceive you. Ask: *How do you know when it is important to be concerned about others' perception, and when it is okay to not worry about what other people think?*

Class Activities

1. Introduce students to the Johari Window (Luft & Ingham, 1955): *The Johari Window is used to help people develop self-awareness and awareness of their relationships with others. The window is meant to allow a person to explore how he or she is perceived within a relationship or context. Discussing the window with a person's family will look different from discussing the window within the contexts of a classroom. It can also be used to understand relationships between two people (peers, coworkers, boss, etc.).*

2. Explain each quadrant to students:
   - **Quadrant 1: Open Area:** What an individual knows about self and is *also* known by others (e.g., "Everyone knows I like basketball, and I'm perceived as witty and compassionate.").
   - **Quadrant 2: Blind Area:** What the individual does not know about self *but* others know (e.g., a person may not know that he or she comes across as arrogant and rude, or that he or she overly interrupts people, but others know.). This may also include strengths and talents others see in the individual, but the individual is not aware of.
   - **Quadrant 3: Hidden Area:** What the individual knows about self that *others do not know* (e.g., "Others do not know that I get my feelings hurt easily. Others do not know that my parents just got a divorce. Others don't know that I can be unkind and rude in other circumstances.").
   - **Quadrant 4: Unknown Area:** What is unknown about self by both individual *and* others (e.g., the aspects of yourself that you don't know exist as traits because you have not had the experiences for these traits to

emerge—Are you a good tennis player (this is not known until the sport is tried)? How would you respond to a major setback in college? What traits would emerge if you tried something out of your comfort zone?

3. Tell students that quadrant sizes can change based on how much is disclosed among individuals (e.g., the Hidden Area gets smaller as a person shares more information within a relationship, causing the Open Area to be bigger). The bigger the Open Area, the more open a relationship is.

4. Divide students into groups of 3–4. Distribute Handout 21.1: Johari Window. Ask students to work through the Open Area quadrant, getting feedback from peers as needed. Students may list interests, personality traits, hobbies, etc. A list of Johari adjectives is also available. Usually 5–6 adjectives are applied to this area of the window.

5. Ask students to quietly think about the Hidden Area and write down ideas of areas that are usually hidden from others. You may ask students to think of something they would not mind sharing with peers; they do not need to get overly personal. Explain that by sharing this with others, it allows this aspect to be moved to the open area, which makes the hidden window smaller.

6. Ask students to look at the "blind spot." Ask: *How is it possible to know what you don't know about yourself?* Explain that it is necessary to seek feedback from other people. Ask: *What risk is there in seeking feedback from others? What feelings might be experienced? How might it be helpful to know about the blind spots? How might this improve interpersonal relationships with others?* Allow students to seek feedback from you or peers, or encourage students to do this on their own time for personal growth. Note that the blind area can shrink when feedback is sought out, which expands the open area. This area is also useful for learning about personal strengths others see, but you may not see.

7. Ask students to look at the Unknown Area. Ask: *How do you know what you don't know about yourself when others don't know either?* One way to know is to try new experiences. Ask: *How does this quadrant relate to ideas of growth mindset and other concepts we have learned about?* Taking risks in new experiences, having the courage to face an unknown obstacle, dealing with the unpleasant emotions of change, and being willing to learn from mistakes are necessary to plunge into understanding this unknown area. Ask students to develop "I wonder" statements about their future (e.g., I wonder how I will be when I am 20, 30, etc.). Then, ask students to consider new challenges they might pursue in the next few weeks to reveal unknown aspects of their life, such as trying a new hobby, sitting by someone different at lunch, etc.

8. (Optional) Ask students to complete a visual for their Johari windows. In each quadrant, students may include symbols, pictures, quotes, etc., to elaborate on how the quadrant relates to their lives. For example, students may

include a picture of a new experience they want to try, a college they may want to go to, and/or a quote about their feelings about the nature of risk in new experiences within the Unknown Area. This may be done with computer graphics or on a program like Glogster. Encourage students to share only what they are comfortable sharing.

Conclusion Connections

Ask: *What emotions are associated with the Open Area . . .the Blind Area. . . the Unknown Area? How can positive emotions be used to fuel a drive for excellence? How might you respond to the discomfort of more unpleasant emotions?* (Remind students of "lean in and push through.") *How does self-awareness catalyze change?*

Curriculum Extension

Ask students to develop a Johari Window for a character from a novel or short story using evidence from the text to support how they develop the window.

Personal Reflection

Have students respond to the following: *What did you learn about yourself from exploring the hidden, blind, and unknown aspects of yourself? How does this exercise relate to developing a drive for excellence?*

Check for Understanding

Have students complete an exit ticket: *If someone is not self-aware of his or her emotional reactions, personal qualities, and how others perceive him or her, how might this affect relationships with others?*

HANDOUT 21.1
Johari Window

Directions: Complete the chart by adding words and experiences that relate to each window for you.

	KNOWN TO SELF	NOT KNOWN TO SELF
Known to Others	Open	Blind Spot
Not Known to Others	Hidden	Unknown

Note. The Johari Window was developed by Luft and Ingram (1955).

A Matter of Perspective

Perspective-taking is critical to students' emotional intelligence. Goleman (2005) pointed to studies asking children or adults to identify the emotion of a provided face; the results showed that accurate emotional recognition in others is indicative of social skill development and behavior management. These skills can be cultivated. We can deliberately teach children to accurately understand who or what is occurring in their world by teaching them to consider perspectives.

Students should be able to examine their own assumptions for a given situation and question those assumptions. Perhaps a student texts a friend about plans for Friday night. Twenty minutes pass without a reply, and our student makes an assumption (i.e., "She must not like me."). But we have to teach students to question personal assumptions. Are there other possibilities beyond the notion that your friend does not like you? Could your friend be in class? Could she be asking permission? Could she have lost her texting privileges? Students should see that the immediate, personal assumption is not always representative of the reality of a situation. There is often more to the story. Students should consider how their assumption colors and shapes resulting emotions (e.g., does the lack of response make you feel angry, disappointed, or confused?). One way to help students with assumption testing is to ask them to think of at least three potential reasons for a behavior they see in others.

A key to enhancing interpersonal relationships is to be able to identify others' points of view and assumptions in a given situation. Bibliotherapy or video therapy are useful tools when teaching interpersonal understanding. Students can read a passage or view a clip of a situation between characters and then respond with their understanding of the situation (e.g., what did each character believe about the situation? What was the true nature (reality) of the situation? How was judgment clouded?). Deliberately considering perspectives allows students to practice these skills so that they can be generalized.

As students consider the perspectives of others, we are truly teaching empathy. Bar-On (2013) defined empathy as the ability to be aware of and understand how others feel. Empathy allows us to interpret how we see others, being sensitive to what, how, and why others may feel as they do. Instead of self-awareness, empathy provides social awareness. When students are working in groups on a large project and one group member has not finished all of her assigned portion, empathy allows other members to consider that this student had to be out of class for 2 days while the family traveled to a relative's funeral. Empathy allows perspective-taking to shape judgment of reality. When students develop empathic perspective-taking, they consider the realities beyond the self. My friend's lack of response may not mean that she does not like me. My peer's lack of work on the project does not mean that she is lazy. In turn, with empathic understanding, truth can be revealed. Students can reflect on their own assumptions and better understand assumptions of others. When we understand each other, we can support each other.

In this lesson, emphasize the second row of the Reframing Thinking Model (see Appendix). Students may question the assumptions and thoughts they are making to move on to taking steps that include empathy and understanding.

Big Idea

Do you see what I see?

Objectives

Students will:
- be able to examine their own assumptions for a given situation and question those assumptions,
- be able to identify others' points of view and assumptions in a given situation, and
- apply the ladder of inference to reflect on their own assumptions and understand assumptions of others.

Materials

- Teacher's copy of *Seven Blind Mice* by Ed Young
- Optical illusion (such as "Square Panel and Circle Illusion," available at https://www.moillusions.com/square-panel-circle-illusion)
- Visual: "Ladder of Inference" developed by Chris Argyris (available online)
- Pair of sunglasses (with the word *assumptions* taped on them)

- Student copies of a fable, such as "The Tortoise and the Hare" by Aesop
- (Optional) Videos: "The Ladder of Inference Creates Bad Judgment" (available at https://www.youtube.com/watch?v=K9nFhs5W8o8) or "Running Up the Ladder of Inference" (available at https://www.youtube.com/watch?v=X7hn4WcGnvA)

Introduction

Read aloud *Seven Blind Mice*. As you read, do not show students the pictures. Ask students to draw what they think is being described. Before getting to the end of the book, which reveals the image as an elephant, ask students to share what they think the "thing" is. Then, reveal that it is an elephant. Ask students: *What does this story reveal about reality? What does this story reveal about perception?*

Class Activities

1. Show students the optical illusion "Square Panel and Circle Illusion." Ask: *Do you see circles or squares?* Students will likely see squares first and eventually the circles. Ask: *Why is it important to understand that people view the world differently?*

2. Explain that when we encounter an issue with other people, everyone brings their own set of beliefs, assumptions, and ideas about a given situation. It is important to be self-aware of our own assumptions and to understand others' points of view and their assumptions. We should carefully think about what we assume about a given situation or a person, consider these assumptions, and then test these assumptions against reality. We all view the world through different "lenses"—demonstrate this by putting on sunglasses. An "assumption" is what we take for granted to be truth. It is like a "story" we tell ourselves about how we see reality.

3. Ask students to read "The Tortoise and the Hare" (or another fable). Ask: *What assumption does the hare make about himself . . . about the tortoise? What "story" does the hare likely tell himself? How is the reality different? How do emotions relate to assumptions we make?*

4. Explain that when we experience negative emotions associated with disappointment or obstacles, one way to manage the emotions is to examine the assumptions we might be making about the given situation. This comes

through self-awareness. This means we take our sunglasses of assumptions off and try to see reality for what it is. Tell students: *You must ask yourself, "What story am I telling myself about the situation?" For example, if you expected to win a competition but didn't, you might tell yourself, "We didn't win because the judges were completely unfair." Once you can identify the "story," or assumption you are making about the situation, then you can start to analyze it. You should start to try to disprove this assumption and think of reasons why it might be wrong (by taking off the sunglasses). Use logic to question your assumptions. For example, "We really didn't get to practice much this past week. The judges had strict guidelines to follow. We were marked down for something that is clearly outlined." By doing this, you are applying logic to your emotions. It is like looking at the situation as if you are a fly on the wall.*

5. Teach students about the "Ladder of Inference" (Argyris, 1990). This model shows how we jump to conclusions automatically about situations. It shows how we develop "stories" from our observations, which lead us to develop inaccurate conclusions. Several versions are available online. We emphasize four main elements of the ladder: observed reality, selected observations, assumptions, and conclusions.

   ■ The ladder rests on *observed reality*. We may observe that a friend did not call us.

   ■ As we move up the ladder, our brains might select aspects of that observation (*selected observations*) to develop assumptions (e.g., we may pay particular attention to how long it has been since a friend sent the text, and this leads to a "story" we tell ourselves).

   ■ We may start to develop the *assumption* (the story we tell ourselves about the situation; e.g., "My friend does not care about me anymore. She's too busy. My text was not important to her.").

   ■ *Conclusion*: To avoid jumping to a conclusion (e.g., "My friend hates me."), it's important to question the assumptions and conclusions. You can go back to the bottom of the ladder and look again at the observed reality. Is there other information that you did not consider? What else could be going on? Explain to students that next time they face an obstacle, challenge, or setback, to be self-aware of how they could erroneously jump to a conclusion.

6. (Optional) Show a video about the ladder of inference (see Materials list).

7. Ask students to apply the assumption testing to the following scenarios. These may be performed as creative skits or with partners. Students can show one scenario showing how assumptions are not questioned and another scenario where assumptions are questioned. Students should refer to elements of the ladder of inference to demonstrate how conclusions are made.

- Your teacher wrote, "See me after class" on your paper.
- You received some critical feedback on your paper and a lower grade than you expected.
- Your friend did not save you a spot at the lunch table.
- Your peer did not do his or her part on the group project.

Conclusion Connections

Refer to the big idea "self-awareness catalyzes change." Ask: *How does this statement relate to the assumptions we make? How do assumptions influence emotions? How might this be an obstacle in pursuing excellence?*

Curriculum Extension

Using a character from any story or novel, have students analyze the assumptions made by that character: *What "story" does the character tell him- or herself about the situation? How are the assumptions different from the reality? How could the character apply the ladder of inference or logic to question assumptions? How would this change the interactions with other characters in the story?*

Personal Reflection

Have students respond to the following: *Think of a time you experienced a conflict, setback, challenge, or obstacle. What assumptions were made about the situation, and/or what stories did you tell yourself to explain the situation? How do emotions influence those assumptions or stories? How might you logically tackle those assumptions?*

Check for Understanding

Ask students to draw a cartoon or make a visual to show an example of questioning assumptions. The visual should show feelings that influence assumptions (or the stories we tell ourselves) and logic to try to disprove the assumption.

Interpersonal Problem Solving

When we understand each other, we can support each other. Bar-On (2006) defined interpersonal relationships as our ability to establish and maintain mutually satisfying relationships and relate well with others. Thus, if we are highly skilled in interpersonal relationships, our relationships will be "win-win;" both parties benefit. Interpersonal relationships are built upon perspective-taking and empathy, two key concepts from Lesson 22. If students are not able to think beyond personal assumptions about others, then interpersonal relationships will be challenging.

A first step in supporting the development of students' interpersonal relationships is assessing the situation with a sociogram, a graphic map that shows direction and connectedness of peer relationships. Sociograms allow teachers to see which students have strong interpersonal networks and which students may need more support. Knowing where your students stand in the classroom social network can be instructive in understanding how students interpret and manage relationships. In many cases, students who lack connected relationships are those who have not developed skills in perspective-taking and empathy. Such students may not listen to others' ideas for the project, or they may shift the conversations and plans to those that are only in line with their ideas. These are not the actions that attract peers to form stronger bonds. It is easily apparent how clashes in assumptions lead to conflict. The lack of perspective-taking results in some students not feeling valued.

Of course, perspective-taking can enhance relationships, and students can be taught prescriptive steps, such as attending to others' interests and needs. A step-by-step plan, such as the PACT strategy from Lessons 7 and 15, can be reworked to support interpersonal problem solving. Students can intentionally think through the problem at hand and the perspectives of those involved. Students are required to consider the needs and preferences of others, which means that they must pay attention to how others view the problem, plausible alternatives, and consequences, not discounting others' ideas or reasons. Students learn to accept and support others. In addition, students are required to consider who benefits from each solution idea. As you work with students in determining solution ideas, guide them to determine who benefits from each decision. In most cases, with some collaboration, multiple people can experience a "win." When students are able to conceptualize solutions that take into account multiple perspectives and preferences, interpersonal growth is happening. Empathy is applied as students consider and infuse multiple perspectives into their group decisions.

Remind students of the Reframing Thinking Model (see Appendix), specifically the second row (thought, challenge the thought, next step). Students may need to view the situation through the other person's perspective and question their own thoughts and assumptions about the situation, moving forward to take next steps that are collaborative.

Big Idea

How can perspective-taking enhance relationships?

Objectives

Students will:

- examine how clashes in assumptions lead to conflict,
- apply perspective-taking to develop skills of empathy, and
- apply problem solving for interpersonal conflicts.

Note. This lesson works best if students understand "assumptions" as introduced in Lesson 22.

Materials

- Handout 23.1: PACT Problem Solving With Point of View
- Video: "The Power of Words: A Girl Changed a Blind Man's Day" (available at https://www.youtube.com/watch?v=QYcXTlGLUgE)

Introduction

1. Ask students to work in pairs. Ask each student to think of a popular song (e.g., "Happy Birthday," "Row, Row, Row Your Boat," etc.; don't let students choose these if you mention them). Have Partner A tap the beat of the song on a desk, and Partner B will try to guess the song. Track how many students are correct. Then, ask Partner B to tap a song, while Partner A tries to guess. Track how many students are correct. Students will likely have a difficult time figuring out the song based only on the rhythm (Heath & Heath, 2007).

2. Ask: *What does this exercise tell us about communication? How does this exercise relate to assumptions?* Guide students to understand that when we communicate and interact with others, we often assume that they are on the same page with us. We assume that they know as much about a situation as we do. We assume that they have an understanding or perspective similar to ours. But their experiences are different from ours because they view situations differently. We don't really know what's in each other's heads.

Class Activities

1. Ask students: *How do assumptions lead to conflicts? How would understanding others' assumptions help increase positive relationships? What examples can you think of when assumptions lead to problems?*

2. Explain to students that it is important to not only understand our own assumptions that we make about situations, but also seek to understand how others think. This enhances interpersonal relationships, collaboration, and leadership skills. As you explain, start yawning. Watch to see if students start yawning because you are yawning and because they see others yawn. Explain that researchers believe that yawning when others yawn is a sign of "empathy"—feeling what others feel. Ask: *When is it easy to relate to how others feel? When is it difficult? What does empathy lead us to do?*

3. Show "The Power of Words: A Girl Changed a Blind Man's Day." Afterward, ask: *Why did people not have empathy at the beginning? What does this video tell us about human nature? What does empathy lead us to do? How do "assumptions" or "the stories we tell ourselves" relate to this video? How do these assumptions relate to empathy?*

4. Explain that understanding others' points of view helps us tackle conflicts. Whenever you are in a conflict with another person, it's often a good idea to see the situation from his or her point of view. Revisit the problem-solving

strategy PACT (Problems, Alternatives, Consequences, Try one) from Lesson 7 and 15. It can also be used to work through conflict with another person. Distribute Handout 23.1: PACT Problem Solving With Point of View. As you explain each step, guide students to consider the assumptions and emotions of each point of view as well as the goal or desire of each point of view. Then, it is important to consider commonalities—what do both groups want?

- **Problem and Point of View:** How does the problem affect each person? What is the problem, and how does each person see the problem? To think deeper, you can analyze the assumptions and emotions behind each perspective. What does each person "want," or what is the goal from that point of view? What do both parties want? What's the commonality?
- **Alternatives:** What are some alternatives/solutions we could explore to solve the problem? How would these alternatives affect both individuals? How would each person think about these alternatives/solutions?
- **Consequences:** What would be the results or consequences of these alternatives? How would the consequences affect each person? What would each person think of these consequences?
- **Try one:** Which alternative should we try? If it doesn't work, start back at A.

5. Explain that developing alternatives in a conflict is often the most difficult. There are various approaches to resolving conflict (win-lose, lose-lose, lose-win, win-win).

6. Guide students with a few examples, referring to Handout 23.1, such as: *You and your project partner cannot decide on an idea for a project in social studies. You want to focus on Renaissance music, but your partner wants to do Renaissance art. Think through PACT:*

- **Problem:** We can't agree. I really love music, play an instrument in the band, and have a strong interest in this topic. My partner enjoys art and is fascinated by da Vinci, especially. We both want a successful project.
- **Alternatives:** Do the project on music (I win, he loses), do the project on art (I lose, he wins), do the project on something entirely different (we both lose), or work toward a combined solution where art and music can be combined in some way (we both give a little, but both win).
- **Consequences:** If we choose music or art, only one person is happy. If we choose to do something entirely different, no one is really happy. If we choose the combined solution, we may have to lower expectations slightly to come to an agreement (Collaboration is working along someone for a common goal where both parties work to a satisfying solution. Compromise is when each person is only partially satisfied in achieving a goal.)
- **Try one!** How did it go?

7. Ask students to think through a personal conflict using the PACT process. Alternatively, you may assign a problem/situation relevant to your classroom/school context or a real-world current event.

Conclusion Connections

Ask: *How does the development of interpersonal skills relate to developing a drive for excellence?* Guide students to understand that in order for them reach high levels of achievement that will undoubtedly encounter conflicts with people. These conflicts may be obstacles that get in the way of pursuing goals. When we understand the assumptions of others, it is easier to problem solve and communicate what we might need for support in attaining those goals.

Curriculum Extension

Have students apply the PACT strategy to a person-versus-person conflict experienced by a character in a short story or novel.

Personal Reflection

Have students respond to the following: *Think through a recent conflict you have experienced. How do you think the other person views the problem? What assumptions do you think the other person has about the issue? How does seeing the situation from his or her point of view help you? Can you think of a win-win solution for the issue?*

Check for Understanding

Have students complete an exit ticket: *How do assumptions lead to conflict? What tips could you offer a friend for dealing with conflict?*

HANDOUT 23.1
PACT Problem Solving With Point of View

Directions: Complete the chart by thinking about a problem, how it affects both people involved, and how it is viewed from two different perspectives.

PERSON 1		PERSON 2
Point of View *Assumptions, thoughts, emotions:*	**Problem**	**Point of View** *Assumptions, thoughts, emotions:*
←→		←→
Goal (I want):	We both want:	Goal (I want):
Point of View *Assumptions, thoughts, emotions:*	**Alternatives and Consequences**	**Point of View** *Assumptions, thoughts, emotions:*
←→		←→
Try One:	↓	

Assuredly Assertive

Assertiveness is key to communicating our needs in a respectful way. But what is it? Bar-On (2013) provided three key elements of assertiveness: an ability to express ourselves on an emotional level, an ability to express ourselves on a cognitive level, and an ability to stand up for personal rights, not letting others take advantage of us. Similar to other facets of emotional intelligence, assertiveness relies on effective self-awareness. Without a full understanding of self, assertiveness is not possible.

Assertive individuals are able to express their feelings and thoughts without destructing relationships or becoming aggressive. They listen to and show respect for others, while also clearly expressing their needs in a respectful way. They tend to have good eye contact and posture and do not allow others to take advantage of them. For example, you may place students into pairs for a large project and provide time in class each week for students to work together. During one of these meeting times, a popular student comes to meet with her partner without her assigned piece completed. If her partner has developed assertiveness skills, then the partner will be able to confront and discuss the situation in a respectful and productive way, perhaps by using "I" messages (e.g., "I know that each of us had an assignment to complete for today, but I noticed that your part has not been finished. I feel that we both have to do our part to make this a successful project. What can we do to make this project process work more effectively?"). But this is not always what happens. Assertive communication is not the default. There are three other basic communication styles that we see in students (and ourselves!):

- **Passive:** Passive communicators refrain from expressing their feelings or thoughts, standing up for their rights, or identifying their feelings. As a result, passive students may be taken advantage of by others. In our example, if the student were a passive communicator, he would likely not confront his

209

partner about her lack of progress even though he feels disappointed or even resentful. Passive students may not have good eye contact, posture, or confident tone, and may experience anxiety surrounding the topic of disappointment because they want to bring an issue up but are too afraid to do so. They fear that confrontation will bring shame, confusion, or regret.

- **Aggressive:** Aggressive communicators openly express their needs and preferences in a way that may violate the feelings or rights of others. These students interrupt, blame, criticize, do not listen to others, and are seen as rude. In the example, if aggressive, he may respond with, "It's all your fault that we are going to fail this assignment. Geez. How hard is it to find three sources for our project?" Aggressive students are not afraid to express how they feel, but they do not consider the perspectives of others. Egocentrism and entitlement may be at work.

- **Passive Aggressive:** Passive aggressive style is "a mixture of passive resistance and grumbling compliance" (Stone, 1993). We see this in students who follow directions, but do so while rolling their eyes or saying "whatever" or "fine" in a sharp tone. Sometimes, individuals exhibiting passive-aggression appear passive to the outside world, but they may look for ways to be uncooperative, seek revenge, or negatively impact the person or situation in question. In the project example, if the student is passive aggressive, he may smile at his peer although he is veiling internal anger. He may feel powerless and resentful in this situation, so he looks for other ways to covertly harm his peer, perhaps by hiding the resources she needs to do her part of the project. It may appear that he is a patient, understanding partner, but this is just a mask to how he truly operates.

Just like adults, students may fear assertive communication and confronting a friend, peer, or even teacher. This is another opportunity to lean in and push through. Students can use assertive communication to facilitate continued progress toward a goal. Assertive communication, or emotional self-expression, is yet another malleable skill that should be practiced and nurtured in the classroom. When you observe a potential conflict, ask students how assertive communication skills could be used to promote a positive outcome. Remind students of the Reframing Thinking Model, guiding students to think about what they can and cannot control in a given situation. One way we can take control of our needs is to use effective communication in interpersonal relationships.

Big Idea

How can I effectively communicate my thoughts, feelings, and needs?

Objectives

Students will:

- apply social awareness skills to given situations (e.g., tactful communication, learning the cultural norm, etc.);
- practice communicating needs and wants in positive, assertive ways; and
- differentiate between aggressive, passive, passive aggressive, and assertive behaviors.

Materials

- Handout 24.1: Communication Styles
- Handout 24.2: Assertive Communication (cut out in advance for groups or pairs)
- (Optional) Snacks and drinks for practicing skills among a social party
- (Optional) Newspapers and tape

Introduction

1. Ask students: *What does it mean to have tact?* Explain that it means having a good sense of knowing how to act or what to say. Discuss with students that this involves being polite, having good manners, not interrupting, following cultural norms, etc.

2. Ask students to share their pet peeves related to interacting with people who lack tact. Develop a class list of dos and don'ts (e.g., don't use cell phones at a restaurant, don't shake people's hands sitting down, look at people in the eyes, use good posture, watch the language you use for the situation, don't dominate a conversation, greet people with their names, use a firm handshake, wear deodorant, etc.). Consider adding to the Tips for Tact list throughout the year.

3. Share the following tip for social savviness: "Observe, then play." Explain: *When other people are playing, talking, or congregating, make observations as to what they are doing and how the conversation is going. First, observe the "cultural rules" of that group, then find an opportunity to test the waters of the group, without dominating or changing the norm. For example, it would be appropriate to ask, "Do you mind if I ask a question about how this works?" or "That's so interesting. Let me see if I understand how you are playing this." This applies to playing games with others, interacting in conversation, at school, etc. (Goleman, 2005).*

4. (Optional) Introduce other practical strategies for building social awareness. Because students are often more engaged with technology than ever before, use this as an opportunity to explicitly teach the skill of pushing through the awkwardness of small talk in social situations. This awkwardness sometimes leads people to bury themselves in technology. Share the following tips. Then, you could ask students to "mingle" as if at a social function. You could even play up the cheesiness for fun with snacks and music.
   - Remember, observe then play (or observe the group, then talk).
   - Always be ready with a question or joke (e.g., have you seen any good movies lately?).
   - Make eye contact.
   - Pay compliments to one another and ask questions about the other person's interests. Seek to find a common interest.
   - Use the person's name in conversation.

Class Activities

1. Ask groups of students to work together to accomplish a team activity. For example, you may ask students in groups of 3–4 to build a tower out of newspaper and tape, where the group with the highest tower wins (the tower cannot fall over). Set a timer for 5–10 minutes and provide no other materials. Afterward, ask: *Did you experience any conflicts? What were your obstacles? What factors contributed to your group's success? How would you rate your communication among team members?* Explain that there are various communication styles people use to communicate their needs and wants. This can vary by context.

2. Refer students to Handout 24.1: Communication Styles, which outlines communication strategies. Emphasize the benefits of assertive communication—communicating needs and wants in a nonthreatening way. You may ask students to explore these types in more depth by reading articles online. Ask students to reflect on the results of each style, including how they affect the other person involved.

3. Explain assertiveness as a form of effective communication. Share the following tips for being assertive while in conflict:
   - Avoid using words like "always" and "never" when in conflict. These words come across as defensive and close communication.
   - Sometimes it's appropriate to agree to disagree.
   - Use assertive body language (eye contact, nod to show that you hear what the person is saying, use open body language without crossed arms, show

confident posture, etc.). Act and speak confidently to firmly express your thoughts as if you really believe they are "true."

- Use an honest and persuasive tone of voice.
- Use active listening. When in a conversation say things like, "What I hear you saying is . . ." or "It sounds like that must be (frustrating, upsetting, etc.)." Ask questions to show that you are interested in listening.

4. Teach students about I-messages—ways to communicate needs in a respectful way, such as saying "I feel _____ when. . . . Would you mind . . . ?" To elaborate further, one might also practice, "I see . . . I thought . . . I felt . . . I want/desire/need. . . ."

5. Share an example response to the first scenario on Handout 24.2: Assertive Communication: *I noticed that we were all assigned a part, but not everyone has brought in their materials. I think that we should all do our part. I feel disappointed that we can't make progress on our project like the other groups. I want us to all do our parts. Jane, can you bring your materials tomorrow or ask (teacher) to allow us to borrow _____ ?*

6. Distribute cutouts from Handout 24.2: Assertive Communication to groups or pairs. Encourage students to use I-messages, active listening, appropriate body language, etc., to develop responses for each of the scenarios.

Conclusion Connections

Ask students: *How do the communication styles relate to having tact? How might these communication strategies affect your pursuit of excellence? How do emotions affect our communication styles? In what ways can you apply "lean in and push through" when interacting with others?*

Curriculum Extension

Have students think about characters in books or stories that would be characterized as having aggressive, assertive, passive-aggressive, and/or passive behaviors: *What evidence suggests they have these communication styles? Choose a character (who acted aggressive, passive-aggressive, or passive) and consider how the plot would have been different if the character acted in an assertive manner. Write out a four-part I-statement (I see,*

I think, I feel, I desire) for a particular part of the book, and explain how it would have affected the conflict, the plot, and/or other characters.

Personal Reflection

Have students respond to the following: *In what relationships or situations do you display aggression, passiveness, and assertiveness? What was the most important thing you learned about communication strategies? Why was this important? What will you now do with this information?*

Check for Understanding

Have students complete an exit ticket: *3-2-1: Write three benefits for expressing your needs assertively. Think of two circumstances in your personal life to which you could apply assertive communication. Write one I-statement that might be relevant to you this week.*

HANDOUT 24.1
Communication Styles

Directions: Complete the chart by thinking about what happens when each communication style is used. Consider how each style might affect relationships with others.

	AGGRESSIVE	ASSERTIVE	PASSIVE	PASSIVE-AGGRESSIVE
Body Language	Hands on hips, index finger pointed forward, lowers eyebrows, rolling eyes.	Open, palms up, confident posture, acts as if things are "true." Direct eye contact.	Slumping. Eyes down.	Eyes roll. Hands up to portray "who cares?"
Thinking	Wants to deliberately hurt others.	Desires understanding.	Insecure. "My thoughts are not important to share."	Denies anger. Wants to get revenge in secret.
Behaviors	Interrupts others. Will take over a group. Speaks loudly.	Participates in groups. Speaks confidently. Takes responsibility.	Afraid to speak. Does not participate in groups. Speaks too softly. Limited responsibility. Whines.	Uses excessive sarcasm and blaming. Chooses to be the victim. Pretends not to care. Cannot be pleased. Refuses to participate. Pretends to forget.
Feelings	Out-of-control anger. Needs power.	Confident.	Powerless. Needs acceptance.	Displaced anger. Unexpressed anger.
Results of Behaviors				

Name:_____ Date: _____

Assertive Communication

Directions: Practice assertiveness for the scenarios.

You are working on a group project. Another person in your group has not done his/her part. This student leaves materials at home and has not done the research for the project. Develop a skit to contrast assertive vs. passive-aggressive behaviors.

You and your friend are having a disagreement on what movie to see. Develop a skit to contrast aggressive vs. assertive behaviors.

You are assigned to work with a partner who is overly bossy and does not allow you to offer ideas or suggestions. Develop a skit to contrast assertive vs. passive behaviors.

Your teacher has made a mistake in grading your paper. This has happened more than once. Develop a skit to contrast assertive vs. passive behaviors.

You are working in a group where others seem to be doing interesting roles, but you are stuck doing something you don't want to do (e.g., researching the information while the others decorate the poster or get on the computer to design something). Develop a skit to contrast assertive vs. passive-aggressive behaviors

References

Adderholdt-Elliott, M. R., & Goldberg, J. (1999). *Perfectionism: What's bad about being so good?* Minneapolis, MN: Free Spirit.

American Psychological Association, Center for Psychology in Schools and Education. (2017). *Top 20 principles from psychology for preK–12 creative, talented, and gifted students' teaching and learning.* Retrieved from http://www.apa.org/ed/schools/teaching-learning/top-principles-gifted.pdf

American Psychological Association, Coalition for Psychology in Schools and Education. (2015). *Top 20 principles from psychology for preK–12 teaching and learning.* Retrieved from http://www.apa.org/ed/schools/cpse/top-twenty-principles.pdf

Antony, M. M., & Swinson, R. P. (2009). *When perfect isn't good enough: Strategies for coping with perfectionism.* Oakland, CA: New Harbinger.

Argyris, C. (1990). The ladder of inference. In P. Senge, *The fifth discipline: The art and practice of the learning organization.* New York, NY: Random House.

Bar-On, R. (1997). *The emotional quotient inventory (EQ-I): A test of emotional intelligence.* Toronto, Canada: Multi-Health Systems.

Bar-On, R. (2006). The Bar-On model of emotional-social intelligence. *Psicothema, 18,* 13–25.

Bar-On, R. (2013). *The 15 factors of the Bar-On model.* Retrieved from http://www.reuvenbaron.org/wp/the-5-meta-factors-and-15-sub-factors-of-the-bar-on-model

Bar-On, R., Maree, J. G., & Elias, M. (2007). *Educating people to be emotionally intelligent.* Westport, CT: Praeger.

Barr, C. (2012). *Deliberate practice: What it is and why you need it* [Web log post]. Retrieved from http://expertenough.com/1423/deliberate-practice

Barseghian, T. (2013). How to foster grit, tenacity and perseverance: An educator's guide. *Mindshift.* Retrieved from https://www.kqed.org/mindshift/27212/how-to-foster-grit-tenacity-and-perseverance-an-educators-guide

Beck, A. T. (1970). Cognitive therapy: Nature and relation to behavior therapy. *Behavior Therapy, 1,* 184–200.

Bloom, B. (1985). *Developing talent in young people.* New York, NY: Ballantine.

Bradberry, T., & Greaves, J. (2009). *Emotional intelligence 2.0.* San Diego, CA: TalentSmart.

Brooks, A. W. (2014). Get excited: Reappraising pre-performance anxiety as excitement. *Journal of Experimental Psychology-General, 143,* 1144–1158. doi:10.1037/a0035325

Compas, B. E., Jaser, S. S., Bettis, A. H., Watson, K. H., Gruhn, M. A., Dunbar, J. P., . . . & Thigpen, J. C. (2017). Coping, emotion regulation, and psychopathology in childhood and adolescence: A meta-analysis and narrative review. *Psychological Bulletin, 143,* 939–991. doi:10.1037/bul0000110

Covey, S. (2004). *The 7 habits of highly effective people.* New York, NY: Free Press.

Coyle, D. (2013). *Introducing the skill-o-meter* [Web log post]. Retrieved from http://danielcoyle.com/2013/10/15/introducing-the-practice-ometer

Csikszentmihalyi, M. (2008). *Flow: The psychology of optimal experience.* New York, NY: HarperCollins.

Deci, E. L., & Ryan, R. M. (2008). Self-determination theory: A macrotheory of human motivation, development, and health. *Canadian Psychology, 49,* 182–185. doi:10.1037/a0012801

Doran, G. T. (1981). There's a S.M.A.R.T. way to write management goals and objectives. *Management Review, 70,* 35–36.

Duckworth, A. (2016). *Grit: The power of passion and perseverance.* New York, NY: Simon & Schuster.

Dweck, C. S. (2000). *Self-theories: Their role in motivation, personality and development.* Philadelphia, PA: Taylor & Francis.

Dweck, C. S. (2006). *Mindset: The psychology of success.* New York, NY: Ballantine Books.

Elliott, A., & Harackiewicz, J. (1996). Approach and avoidance achievement goals and intrinsic motivation: A mediational analysis. *Journal of Personality and Social Psychology, 70,* 461–475.

Ellis, A. (1962). *Reason and emotion in psychotherapy.* New York, NY: Stuart.

Ericsson, A., & Pool, R. (2016). *Peak: Secrets from the new science of expertise.* Boston, MA: Houghton Mifflin Harcourt.

Fogarty, R. J., Kerns, G. M., & Pete, B. M. (2018). *Unlocking student talent: The new science of developing expertise.* New York, NY: Teachers College Press.

Frost, R. O., Marten, P., Lahart, C., & Rosenblate, R. (1990). The dimensions of perfectionism. *Cognitive Therapy and Research, 14,* 449–468.

Gallwey, T. (1997). *The inner game of tennis: A classic guide to the mental side of peak performance.* New York, NY: Random House.

Goleman, D. (2005). *Emotional intelligence: Why it can matter more than IQ.* New York, NY: Bantam.

Gottfredson, L. S. (1997). Mainstream science on intelligence: An editorial with 52 signatories, history, and bibliography. *Intelligence, 24,* 13–23.

Greenspon, T. (2016, November). Helping gifted students move beyond perfectionism. *Teaching for High Potential,* 10–12.

Grunschel, C., Patrzek, J., & Fries, S. (2013). Exploring reasons and consequences of academic procrastination: An interview study. *European Journal of Psychology of Education, 28,* 841–861. doi:10.1007/s10212-012-0143-4

Hamachek, D. E. (1978). Psychodynamics of normal and neurotic perfectionism. *Psychology, 15,* 27–33.

Heath, C., & Heath, D. (2007). *Made to stick: Why some ideas survive and others die.* New York, NY: Random House.

Hidi, S., & Renninger, K. A. (2006). The four-phased model of interest development. *Educational Psychologist, 41,* 111–127.

Jamieson, J. P., Mendes, W., Blackstock, E., & Schmader, T. (2010). Turning the knots in your stomach into bows: Reappraising arousal improves performance on the GRE. *Journal of Experimental Social Psychology, 46,* 208–212. doi:10.1016/j.jesp.2009.08.015

Keller, A., Litzelman, K., Wisk, L. E., Maddox, T., Cheng, E. R., Creswell, P. D., & Witt, W. P. (2012). Does the perception that stress affects health matter? The association with health and mortality. *Health Psychology, 31,* 677–684. doi:10.1037/a0026743

Luciani, J. (2015). Why 80 percent of New Year's resolutions fail. *U.S. News and World Report.* Retrieved from https://health.usnews.com/health-news/blogs/eat-run/articles/2015-12-29/why-80-percent-of-new-years-resolutions-fail

Luft, J., & Ingham, H. (1955). *The Johari Window: A graphic model for interpersonal relations.* University of California-Los Angeles Western Training Lab.

Marsh, H. (1984). Self-concept: The application of a frame of reference model to explain paradoxical results. *Australian Journal of Education, 28,* 165–181.

Mischel, W. (2014). *The marshmallow test: Mastering self-control.* New York, NY: Little, Brown.

Mischel, W., Shoda, Y., Rodriguez. M. (1989). Delay of gratification in children. *Science, 244,* 933–938.

Mofield, E. (2008). *The effects of an affective curriculum on perfectionism and coping in gifted middle school students* (Doctoral dissertation). Tennessee State University, Nashville, TN.

Mofield, E., & Parker Peters, M. (2015). Multidimensional perfectionism within gifted adolescents: An exploration of typology and comparison of samples. *Roeper Review, 37,* 97–109.

Mofield, E., & Parker Peters, M. (2018a). Mindset misconception? Comparing mindsets, perfectionism, and attitudes of achievement in gifted, advanced, and typical students. *Gifted Child Quarterly, 62,* 327–349. https://doi.org/10.1177/0016986218758440

Mofield, E., & Parker Peters, M. (2018b). Shifting the perfectionist's mindset: Moving toward mindful excellence. *Gifted Child Today, 41,* 177–185.

Mofield, E., Parker Peters, M., & Chakraborti-Ghosh, S. (2016). Perfectionism, coping, and underachievement in gifted adolescents: Avoidance vs. approach orientations. *Educational Sciences, 6,* 1–22. doi:10.3390/educsci6030021

Oettingen, G. (2015). *Rethinking positive thinking: Inside the new science of motivation.* New York, NY: Penguin.

Oettingen, G., & Gollwitzer, P. M. (2010). Strategies of setting and implementing goals: Mental contrasting and implementation intentions. In J. E. Maddux & J. P. Tangney (Eds.), *Social psychological foundations of clinical psychology* (pp.114–135). New York, NY: Guilford Press.

Oettingen, G., Kappes, H. B., Guttenberg, K. B., & Gollwitzer, P. M. (2015). Self-regulation of time management: Mental contrasting with implementation intentions. *European Journal of Social Psychology, 45,* 218–229. doi:10.1002/ejsp.2090

Olszewski-Kubilius, P., & Calvert, E. (2016). Implications of the talent development framework for curriculum design. In T. Kettler (Ed.), *Modern curriculum for gifted and advanced academic students* (pp. 37–54). Waco, TX: Prufrock Press.

Olszewski-Kubilius, P., & Clarenbach, J. (2012). *Unlocking emergent talent: Supporting high achievement of low-income, high-ability students.* Washington, DC: National Association for Gifted Children.

Parker Peters, M., & Mofield, E. (2017). Mindsets matter for gifted children. *Parenting for High Potential, 6,* 4–9.

Paunesku, D., Walton, G. M., Romero, C., Smith, E. N., Yeager, D. S., & Dweck, C. S. (2015). Mind-set interventions are a scalable treatment for academic underachievement. *Psychological Sciences, 26,* 784–793. doi:10.1177/0956797615571017

Plutchik, R. & Kellerman, H. (1980). *Emotion: Theory, research, and experience: Vol. 1. Theories of emotion.* New York, NY: Academic Press.

Ramsey, D., & Ramsey, P. (2002). Reframing the perfectionist's catch-22 dilemma: A systems thinking approach. *Journal for the Education of the Gifted, 26,* 99–112.

Renzulli, J. S. (1986), The three-ring conception of giftedness: A developmental model for creative productivity. In R. J. Sternberg & J. E. Davidson (Eds.), *Conceptions of giftedness* (pp. 53–92). New York, NY: Cambridge University Press.

Roth, S., & Cohen, L. J. (1986). Approach, avoidance, and coping with stress. *American Psychologist, 41,* 813–819. doi:10.1037/0003-066X.41.7.813

Saarni, C. (1999). *The development of emotional competence.* New York, NY: Guilford Press.

Seligman, M. (2006). *Learned optimism: How to change your mind and your life.* New York, NY: Vintage Books.

Seligman, M., & Csikszentmihalyi, M. (2000). Positive psychology: An introduction. *American Psychologist, 55,* 5–14. doi:10.1037//0003-066X.55.1.5

Siegle, D., & McCoach, B. (2005). Making a difference: Motivating gifted students who are not achieving. *Teaching Exceptional Children, 38,* 22–27.

Snyder, C. R. (2000). Hypothesis: There is hope. In C. R. Snyder (Eds.), *Handbook of hope theory, measures and applications* (pp. 3–21). San Diego, CA: Academic Press.

Snyder, C. R., Shorey, H. S., Cheavens, J., Pulvers, K. M., Adams, V. H., & Wiklund, C. (2002). Hope and academic success in college. *Journal of Educational Psychology, 94,* 820–826. doi:10.1037//0022-0663.94.4.820

Steel, P. (2007). The nature of procrastination: A meta-analytic and theoretical review of quintessential self-regulatory failure. *Psychological Bulletin, 133,* 65–94.

Stone, M. (1993). *Abnormalities of personality: Within and beyond the realm of treatment.* New York, NY: Norton.

Subotnik, R. F. (2015). Psychological strength training: The missing piece in talent development. *Gifted Child Today, 38,* 41–48.

Subotnik, R. F., & Jarvin, L. (2005). Beyond expertise: Conceptions of giftedness as great performance. In R. J. Sternberg & J. Davidson (Eds.), *Conceptions of giftedness* (2nd ed., pp. 343–357). New York, NY: Cambridge University Press.

Subotnik, R. F., Olszewski-Kubilius, P., & Worrell, F. C. (2011). Rethinking giftedness and gifted education: A proposed direction forward based on psychological science. *Psychological Science in the Public Interest, 12,* 3–54. doi:10.1177/1529100611418056

Taylor, J. B. (2009). *My stroke of insight: A brain scientist's personal journey.* New York, NY: Penguin Books.

Torrance, E. P. (1974). *Torrance Tests of Creative Thinking.* Bensonville, IL: Scholastic Testing Service.

VanTassel-Baska, J. (2009). *Affective curriculum and instruction for gifted learners.* In J. VanTassel-Baska, T. Cross, & F. R. Olencheck (Eds.), *Social-emotional curriculum with gifted and talented students* (pp. 113–132). Waco, TX: Prufrock Press.

Voge, D. (2007). Classroom resources for addressing procrastination. *Research and Teaching in Developmental Education, 23,* 88–96.

Webb, J., Amend, E., Webb, N., Goerss, J., Beljan, P., & Olenchak, F. R. (2005). *Misdiagnosis and dual diagnoses of gifted children and adults: ADHD, bipolar, OCD, Asperger's, depression, and other disorders.* Scottsdale, AZ: Great Potential Press.

Weiner, B. (1974). *Achievement motivation and attribution theory.* Morriston, NJ: General Learning Press.

Whitehead, A. N. (1929). *The aims of education and other essays.* New York, NY: Macmillan.

Yerkes, R., & Dodson, J. (1908). The relation of strength of stimulus to rapidity of habit formation. *Journal of Comparative and Neurological Psychology, 18,* 459–482.

Appendix:
Additional Resources and
Supplemental Lesson

Reframing Thinking Model

	Self-awareness	Management Strategies	Outcomes
Context	Situation	Filter: What is out of your control?	What is within your control?
Logic	Thought assumptions	Challenge the thought	Next step
Emotions	Emotions/feelings/ physical reactions	Use a coping strategy	Regulated emotion

Webpage Resources

Several additional resources are available on the book's webpage (https://www.prufrock.com/teaching-tenacity-resources.aspx), including:

- **Extended Reflections for Gifted Students:** The webpage includes extended reflections for gifted students, which provide questions, activities, and additional ideas for relating giftedness to many of the lessons. Activities also align well with the National Association for Gifted Children Gifted Programming Standards for Grades K–12, specifically self-understanding, awareness of needs, and cognitive and affective growth.
- **Underachievement Connections:** Many ideas and lessons in this curriculum can be used to address motivational issues with underachievers. The webpage includes a list that details lesson connections related to underachievement.
- **Lesson 25: Understanding Giftedness:** The supplemental lesson available on the webpage guides gifted students to become aware of how their exceptional abilities affect their thoughts, emotions, and beliefs about their abilities.

About the Authors

Emily Mofield, Ed.D., is an assistant professor in the College of Education at Lipscomb University. Her background includes 15 years experience teaching gifted students and leading gifted services. Emily currently serves as the National Association for Gifted Children (NAGC) Chair for Curriculum Studies. She is a National Board Certified Teacher in language arts and has been recognized as the Tennessee Association for Gifted Children Teacher of the Year. She has been recognized with numerous NAGC curriculum awards for coauthored units with Tamra Stambaugh (*Space, Structure, and Story* [2017], *I, Me, You, We: Individuality Versus Conformity* [2016], *Perspectives of Power* [2015], and *In the Mind's Eye: Truth Versus Perception* [2012]). She has authored several research articles on the social-emotional needs of gifted students and has received the NAGC Hollingworth Award for excellence in research (with Megan Parker Peters). Emily regularly presents professional development addressing the social-emotional needs of gifted learners and implementing effective differentiation strategies for advanced learners for school districts and special groups.

Megan Parker Peters, Ph.D., is an associate professor and the Director of Teacher Education and Assessment at Lipscomb University. She is also a psychologist, specializing in the needs of gifted and twice-exceptional learners. She is the current chair of the Early Childhood Network of NAGC. Megan is the past president of the Tennessee Association of the Gifted and currently serves on its board. Megan is the recipient of the 2017 Jo Patterson Award for long-term dedication to gifted education and advocacy in the state of Tennessee. She has authored or coauthored several research articles concerning the social and academic needs of gifted students. She is also the recipient of NAGC's Hollingworth Award for research on achievement motivation (with Emily Mofield).

NAGC Programming Standards Alignment

LESSONS	STUDENT OUTCOMES	EVIDENCE-BASED PRACTICES
Pre- and post-assessment; Lessons 1–3, 21; Lesson 25 (online)	**1.1. Self-Understanding.** Students with gifts and talents demonstrate self-knowledge with respect to their interests, strengths, identities, and needs in socio-emotional development and in intellectual, academic, creative, leadership, and artistic domains.	1.1.1. Educators engage students with gifts and talents in identifying interests, strengths, and gifts.
		1.1.2. Educators assist students with gifts and talents in developing identities supportive of achievement.
Pre- and postassessment; Lessons 1–10, 18, 19, 21; Lesson 25 (online)	**1.2. Self-Understanding.** Students with gifts and talents possess a developmentally appropriate understanding of how they learn and grow; they recognize the influences of their beliefs, traditions, and values on their learning and behavior.	1.2.1. Educators develop activities that match each student's developmental level and culture-based learning needs.

LESSONS	STUDENT OUTCOMES	EVIDENCE-BASED PRACTICES
Lessons 18–19, 21–24; Lesson 25 (online)	**1.3. Self-Understanding.** Students with gifts and talents demonstrate understanding of and respect for similarities and differences between themselves and their peer group and others in the general population.	1.3.1. Educators provide a variety of research-based grouping practices for students with gifts and talents that allow them to interact with individuals of various gifts, talents, abilities, and strengths.
		1.3.2. Educators model respect for individuals with diverse abilities, strengths, and goals.
Lessons 2–3, 10, 24; Lesson 25 (online)	**1.4. Awareness of Needs.** Students with gifts and talents access resources from the community to support cognitive and affective needs, including social interactions with others having similar interests and abilities or experiences, including same-age peers and mentors or experts.	1.4.1. Educators provide role models (e.g., through mentors, bibliotherapy) for students with gifts and talents that match their abilities and interests.
Lessons 4–5, 7, 11–15, 17, 20; Lesson 25 (online)	**1.6. Cognitive and Affective Growth.** Students with gifts and talents benefit from meaningful and challenging learning activities addressing their unique characteristics and needs.	1.6.1. Educators design interventions for students to develop cognitive and affective growth that is based on research of effective practices.
		1.6.2. Educators develop specialized intervention services for students with gifts and talents who are underachieving and are now learning and developing their talents.

LESSONS	STUDENT OUTCOMES	EVIDENCE-BASED PRACTICES
Lessons 2–3, 6, 19, 21–23; Lesson 25 (online)	**1.8. Cognitive and Affective** Growth. Students with gifts and talents identify future career goals that match their talents and abilities and resources needed to meet those goals (e.g., higher education opportunities, mentors, financial support).	1.8.2. Teachers and counselors implement a curriculum scope and sequence that contains person/social awareness and adjustment, academic planning, and vocational and career awareness.
Lessons 2–4, 7–9, 11, 14, 18–21; Lesson 25 (online)	**3.2. Talent Development.** Students with gifts and talents become more competent in multiple talent areas and across dimensions of learning.	3.2.1. Educators design curricula in cognitive, affective, aesthetic, social, and leadership domains that are challenging and effective for students with gifts and talents.
		3.2.2. Educators use meta-cognitive models to meet the needs of students with gifts and talents.
		3.3.3. Educators provide opportunities for students with gifts and talents to explore, develop, or research their areas of interest and/or talent.
All lessons	**4.1. Personal Competence.** Students with gifts and talents demonstrate growth in personal competence and dispositions for exceptional academic and creative productivity. These include self-awareness, self-advocacy, self-efficacy, confidence, motivation, resilience, independence, curiosity, and risk taking.	4.1.2. Educators provide opportunities for self-exploration, development and pursuit of interests, and development of identities supportive of achievement, e.g., through mentors and role models.
		4.1.3. Educators create environments that support trust among diverse learners.

LESSONS	STUDENT OUTCOMES	EVIDENCE-BASED PRACTICES
All lessons, *continued*		4.1.4. Educators provide feedback that focuses on effort, on evidence of potential to meet high standards, and on mistakes as learning opportunities.
		4.1.5. Educators provide examples of positive coping skills and opportunities to apply them.
Lessons 14–15, 18–19. 21–24; Lesson 25 (online)	**4.2. Social Competence.** Students with gifts and talents develop social competence manifested in positive peer relationships and social interactions.	4.2.3. Educators assess and provide instruction on social skills needed for school, community, and the world of work.
Lessons 1–6, 14–15, 19, 21–24, Lesson 25 (online)	**4.3. Leadership**. Students with gifts and talents demonstrate personal and social responsibility and leadership skills.	4.3.1 Educators establish a safe and welcoming climate for addressing social issues and developing personal responsibility.
		4.3.2. Educators provide environments for developing many forms of leadership and leadership skills.
Lessons 22–24	**4.4. Cultural Competence.** Students with gifts and talents value their own and others' language, heritage, and circumstance. They possess skills in communicating, teaming, and collaborating with diverse individuals and across diverse groups. They use positive strategies to address social issues, including discrimination and stereotyping.	4.4.3. Educators provide structured opportunities to collaborate with diverse peers on a common goal.

LESSONS	STUDENT OUTCOMES	EVIDENCE-BASED PRACTICES
Lessons 2, 4–8; Lesson 25 (online)	**5.7. Career Pathways**. Students with gifts and talents identify future career goals and the talent development pathways to reach those goals.	5.7.1. Educators provide professional guidance and counseling for individual student strengths, interests, and values.